Jane Coe Smith

COLLEGE STUDENT
MENTAL HEALTH

NASPA

Student Affairs Administrators
in Higher Education

COLLEGE STUDENT MENTAL HEALTH

Effective Services and Strategies Across Campus

EDITED BY

Sherry A. Benton
& Stephen L. Benton

NASPA
Student Affairs Administrators
in Higher Education

College Student Mental Health:
Effective Services and Strategies Across Campus

Additional copies may be purchased by contacting the NASPA publications department at 301-638-1749 or visiting http://www.naspa.org/publications.

ISBN 0-931654-45-9

CONTENTS

CHAPTER 1

The Scope and Context of the Problem

Sherry A. Benton

*I*t's 8:30 on Monday morning and I'm at the weekly counseling *center staff meeting catching up on what has been an eventful weekend on campus. During the past three days a student named Anne stood up and disrupted her biology class, stood in the middle of a busy city street and screamed obscenities for over a half hour, and stayed up all night talking about conspiracies and grave dangers on campus and frightening her roommate. Before that, she had disrupted other classes, behaved bizarrely in her residence hall complex, and seemed to go days without sleep. The after-hours counselor on duty called her former psychiatrist and learned some* *helpful background information. Anne had a history of bipolar disorder with psychotic features. She had been doing well under good psychiatric care, but now refused to take her medications. Until this semester, Anne had seemed a bit eccentric, but she had functioned adequately and received good grades.*

The vice president for institutional advancement, assistant dean of student life, an academic advisor, Anne's parents, the residence hall and health center staffs, campus police, city police, classmates, and neighbors have now all become involved, along with the counseling center staff. The counseling center has policies and procedures for these matters, and all concerned quickly decide that Anne needs to be disenrolled for reasons of mental health and to be removed from campus. Her parents have been through this ordeal too many times and are too worn out to be of much help. They have no interest in having her move home. The winter cold raises concerns about where to send her. She is not a danger to herself or others so there are no legal grounds to hospitalize her involuntarily. She refuses to go in on her own. The local shelter will not take people who are having psychotic symptoms. In this small community, all psychiatrists are completely booked and not taking new patients. Professionals at the local community mental health center do what they can, but they are overwhelmed as well. At our staff meeting, my colleagues and I try to think of any other options for ensuring her well-being and safety at the same time that we are getting her out of school to preserve the academic environment for everyone else. At this point, our counseling center staff has spent about 50 hours on this particular student.

Figure 1.1. The Story of Anne.

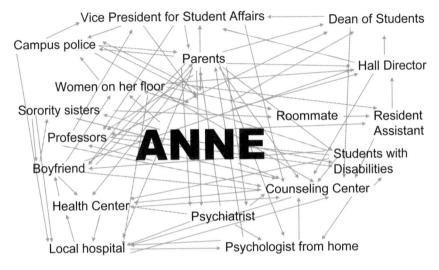

Source: Author compilation.

This is only one of many students with serious mental health problems seen on college and university campuses every year. Multiply Anne's situation by the thousands of campuses across the United States and it is clear that college and university personnel face a large problem that consumes tens of thousands of hours of faculty and staff time.

In the past few years, 85% of counseling center directors have reported seeing more students with serious mental health problems than they had the previous five years (Gallagher, Gill, & Sysco, 2000). In a 2002 survey of 16,000 students on 28 campuses, the American College Health Association found that 54.6% of students reported feeling hopeless in the past year, 37.6% reported feeling so depressed three or more times in the past year that they could not function, 9.5% reported seriously considering suicide in the previous year, and 1.4%

reported attempting suicide in the previous year. In research conducted at Kansas State University during the course of 13 years examining changes in college student mental health problems, my colleagues and I found that the proportions of students seen for anxiety disorders doubled, depression tripled, and serious suicidal ideation and intent tripled (Benton, Robertson, Tseng, Newton, & Benton, 2003). The ubiquitous nature of the problem was clear in the sheer volume of attention that this study—conducted on one campus in the middle of the central prairie—received. We participated in more than 150 interviews with the national and international press, were invited to present at several professional conferences, and talked with dozens of campus officials across the United States. We heard consistently that college student mental health problems are becoming more common, more problematic, and a much larger focus on college and university campuses.

College student mental health problems are not new. In 1918, the dean of students at Harvard University reported that student mental health problems were the number one health challenge to college and university administrators (Williamson, 1961). Although the problems haven't changed, the context, prevalence, and expectations of the institution have changed dramatically. To understand how college student mental health problems and expectations of college and university staff and administrators have changed, it is helpful to review the history and context of the problem.

Changes in the Relationship Between the Student and the Institution

Throughout the history of American colleges and universities, the relationship between the student and the institution has changed dramatically, with the preponderance of change occurring within the last 40 years. From the 1700s through the 1950s, students were primarily viewed as adolescents whose unruly tendencies needed to be controlled. Universities were viewed *in loco parentis* and had wide latitude in regulating and managing student behavior. From the 1960s through the 1980s, students' rights and freedom were established through a series of court cases. *Dixon vs. Alabama State Board of Education*, 1961, (294 F.2d 150) successfully abolished the concept of *in loco parentis*. Following this several Supreme Court rulings established that students over the age of 18 were adults and had the right to make their own decisions (Bickel and Lake, 1994). Universities had far less capacity to regulate students and were not held responsible for most misbehavior. In the last decade, the relationship between student and institution has again shifted. As students and parents have shouldered more of the financial burden of paying for school, with less legislative support even for state schools, more families have come to look at their relationship to the college or university from a consumer perspective. The college or university is the vendor, trying to sell them a product, and they are the consumer buying an education. Public demand for information about retention rates, graduation rates, graduate employment patterns, and safety issues on campus have become ubiquitous (Nuss, 2003). All of this information is seen as essential in allowing families to purchase the best education possible. Parents tend to view problems that their student encounters as the institution's failure to deliver the quality of product they thought they had purchased. In our conversations with dozens of individuals on college and university campuses, many student affairs officers noted increases in phone calls from parents addressing issues problematic for the student. The result is that college and university personnel have less control over student behavior than they had in the past but face much higher expectations from parents for both managing student behavior and providing high-quality student services, including counseling and mental health services.

CHANGES IN SOCIETAL EXPECTATIONS OF THE INSTITUTION: UNIVERSITY LIABILITY AND LAWSUITS

Many college and university administrators were alarmed when a Massachusetts Superior Court judge ruled in July 2005 that the parents of a Massachusetts Institute of Technology (MIT) student who committed suicide at the school could proceed with their $27 million lawsuit against school administrators and staff (Hoover, 2005). Non-clinicians had not typically been held responsible for preventing suicide, but in this case, a dean of student life and a residence hall director were held accountable along with psychiatrists and mental health professionals at MIT. This precedent is particularly worrisome as college and university personnel ponder their responsibility for the behavior of students with mental health problems and suicidal risk, whose numbers are increasing on campuses. Many student affairs administrators fear that they will face costly litigation following a student suicide, particularly because suicide is the second leading cause of death in the 18–24 age group.

Public Expectations

Sunshine laws in the 1980s and early 1990s increased public access to information about the inner functioning of universities, and this led to greater public scrutiny and expectations that campus administrators should regulate and manage student problems. A generation ago, students were held accountable for their own behavior. Today, college and university personnel are regularly asked about how they are managing campus problems such as alcohol use or student suicide risk.

Changes in Students

Brown vs. the Board of Education of Topeka, the 1964 Civil Rights Act, Title IX in 1972, and the Americans with Disabilities Act in 1990 have all contributed to changing the make-up of student populations and providing opportunities for higher education for more citizens. Today's students are:

* More diverse

* More often women

* More first generation

* More foreign born

* More nontraditional

With these changes in the student body, campuses may need to address issues of acceptance and dealing with differences. The unique needs and pressures on this changing student body are an important consideration.

Changes in Families and Communications

A generation ago, the common form of communication between a student and his or her parents was the once weekly, Sunday evening phone call. I remember this as one of my planned weekly events. For students at that time, a long-distance phone call was expensive, and they needed to use the time efficiently because students living away from home could not otherwise communicate with their parents.

In contrast, today's students can contact their parents through e-mail, cell phones, and text messaging whenever they please. This increase in communication inevitably leads to more involvement of parents in a student's day-to-day problems. Parents expect more involvement and may be frustrated by laws about confidentiality, HIPAA (the Health Insurance Portability and Accountability Act of 1996), and FERPA (the Family Educational Rights and Privacy Act). Student affairs administrators report spending far more time dealing with parents today than in past years (Strauss, 2006). This may be particularly true for a student with mental health concerns.

WHY ARE MENTAL HEALTH PROBLEMS MORE PREVALENT AMONG STUDENTS?

There is no simple answer to this question. Prevalence studies can document that a trend is happening but they cannot determine causes. Psychologists can, however, speculate about factors that might affect mental health problems among students. Because these factors vary widely among students, it is most meaningful to describe several hypothetical cases.

Angie is a 20-year-old sophomore in pre-medicine. She has a 3.95 GPA on a 4.0 scale and is taking mostly hard science courses. She is active in a sorority on campus and functions at a high level most of the time. She has referred herself to the counseling center because she is beginning to have a re-occurrence of symptoms of obsessive-compul-

sive disorder (OCD). She finds herself checking and rechecking to see that she has unplugged her iron, she drives around the block exactly three times before she can park her car, and she fears that something terrible will happen if she does not follow her rituals. Angie was first diagnosed with OCD in elementary school. She has two aunts and a cousin who have OCD. Over the years she has taken medication and learned some strategies to minimize symptoms, preventing them from interfering with her functioning in school and with friends and family. She has had occasional short re-occurrences of symptoms when her stress levels become too high, or when she changes her medication. She makes good use of short-term counseling and medication consultation to return to her usual high levels of achievement.

Angie is an example of a successful resolution of a mental health problem. She was diagnosed early, treated appropriately, and, as a result, has achieved at a high level and manages her disorder with only minimal problems. A generation ago, the medications Angie now finds effective were not available, and psychologists knew little about what sorts of therapy would be most effective. In that previous generation, OCD symptoms might have prevented someone like Angie from ever getting to college. Now, with better treatment, students like her can thrive in college and in their careers. Many students with mental health problems arrive on campus having already received medication. Effective early therapy has enabled them to reach college and to achieve good academic success. These students often need some continued medication consultation, relapse prevention, and support to succeed in college and university settings.

Zeke is a 21-year-old senior in electrical engineering. Early in his educational experience, he had been an A student with only an occasional B since grade school. He had been a high achiever who took leadership roles in several clubs and organizations and had performed very well on two internships in the past couple of years. He had also worked a part time job through most of his undergraduate years. Each year of college, he took on more responsibilities and activities. He felt stressed by the end of his sophomore year. In spite of this, he cut out some sleep and meal times to make room for these additional professional activities. By the end of his sophomore year, he had developed several symptoms of an anxiety disorder, including restlessness, fatigue, difficulty concentrating, difficulty sleeping, irritability, and muscle tension. He found himself worrying all the time about not getting things done and performing poorly. During a summer internship he knew something was very wrong. He was struggling to stay motivated and seemed to stop caring about himself or his future. Early in the fall of his senior year, he collapsed into major depression. He felt depressed nearly every day. He stopped attending classes, stayed in bed all day, lost all interest in activities, lost his appetite, lost weight, felt fatigued and worthless, and had no ability to concentrate. Within a few months he was ruminating about death and began to imagine how he could commit suicide. Finally, at this low point, he sought help from the counseling center.

Zeke is an example of a student who college and university therapists see all too often. Students like him represent a large number of the kinds of students counseling centers see. They seem to feel more pressure and urgency about achieving than students might have felt 10 or 15 years ago. They start out expecting perfection of themselves and feel as if they have failed if they don't achieve at their often unrealistic standards. Zeke ignored basic self-care and lived without any balance in his life, which caused some serious problems over time. A counseling center therapist would start by immediately addressing the suicide risk and then treating the depression. Long term, it is important for students like Zeke to attend to self-care and to learn to achieve at a high level without the perfectionist "all-or-nothing" thinking that leaves them feeling dissatisfied with everything they do.

Darren is a 25-year-old sophomore in arts and sciences. His academic performance has been inconsistent, with grades ranging from A to F. When he performs well academically, he feels like an imposter; when he does poorly he is wracked with self-doubt and self-blame. Darren frequently feels angry and alienated. He struggles to trust others and to feel hope about his future. His stepfather appears to be an alcoholic and was frequently violent in Darren's youth. His mother was too overwhelmed to provide much support or protection for him. His advisor, who was concerned about his inconsistent academic performance, referred Darren to the counseling center. He came in complaining about his lack of motivation and his irritability.

Darren is another sort of student frequently seen in a college or university counseling center. He appears to have a significant history of trauma, abuse, and neglect in his family. This has led to difficulty functioning in his adult life. When students leave home for college, it is frequently the first time they feel free to pursue counseling apart from their parents.

In summary, there are a wide variety of factors that seem to be leading to increases in mental health problems among students. In some cases improvements in treatment, medications, and understanding of mental disorders have made higher education more attainable for many people with psychological disorders. In other cases, increased pressure, perfectionism, and decreased social support and self-care have lead to increases in disorders such as anxiety and depression. Along with these factors, other issues in the culture, such as family dysfunction, can lead to psychological problems.

What Can Be Done to Address the Problem?

The editors' goals in compiling the chapters of this book are to:

1. Help college and university administrators gain an understanding of the scope of mental health problems on campuses.

2. Help college and university administrators understand the legal issues associated with students with mental health problems.

3. Provide theoretical frameworks and practical strategies for supplying comprehensive and integrated services for students with mental health problems.

4. Provide more specific theory, strategies, and ideas for relevant student affairs offices.

5. Help administrators understand the unique needs of some populations on campus.

The following chapters focus on finding effective strategies to address problems of college student mental health from a variety of directions. In Chapter 2, Owen, Tao, and Rodolfa discuss comprehensive, campus-wide strategies for dealing with mental health issues. These authors suggest the "cube model" (Morrill et al., 1974, and Moore and Delworth, 1976) as a theoretical framework for organizing inter-departmental collaboration. In Chapter 3, Dickerson presents a very helpful summary of legal issues associated with student mental health problems. She describes implementation of a Facilitator Model (Bickel and Lake, 1999) as a vision for understanding the integration of law and policy on college campuses. Benton, Benton, and Perl discuss issues and strategies for faculty members in dealing with students mental health problems in Chapter 4. In Chapter 5, Newton focuses on crisis intervention and the application of the cube model and the Assessment-Intervention of Student Problems model (Delworth, 1989) to crisis intervention. In Chapter 6, Cooper examines the major issues and challenges facing college mental health centers. In Chapter 7, Osfield and Junco describe the role of students with disabilities offices in helping students with mental health disabilities succeed. In Chapter 8, Moses presents the role of health centers in working with students with mental health problems. In Chapter 9, Brent, Cornish, Leslie-Toogood, Nadkarni, and Schreier discuss college student mental health and special populations on campus. In Chapter 10, Benton and Benton stress the importance of addressing student mental health needs and summarize strategies for campus response.

REFERENCES

Benton, S. A., Benton, S. L., Newton, F. B., Benton, K. L., & Robertson, J. M. (2004). Changes in client problems: Contributions and limitations from a 13-year study. *Professional Psychology: Research and Practice, 35*, 317-319.

Bickel, R. D., & Lake, P. T. (1994). Reconceptualizing the university's duty to provide a safe learning environment: A criticism of the doctrine of *in loco parentis* and the restatement (second) of torts. *Journal of College and University Law, 20*, 261-293.

Hoover, E. (2005, August 12). Judge rules suicide suit against MIT can proceed. *Chronicle of Higher Education.* Retrieved April 3, 2006 from http://chronicle.com/free/v51/i49/49a00101.htm

Nuss, E. M. (2003). The development of student affairs. In S.R. Komives, S.R. and Woodard, D. B. (Eds.), *Student Services: A Handbook for the Profession,* fourth edition. San Francisco: Jossey-Bass.

Strauss, V. (2006, March 21). Putting parents in their place: Outside of class. *Washington Post*, Retrieved April 3, 2006 from http://www.washingtonpost.com/wp-dyn/content/article/2006/03/20/AR2006032001167_pf.html

Williamson, E. G. (1961). *Student Personnel Services in Colleges and Universities.* New York: McGraw-Hill.

CHAPTER 2

Distressed and Distressing Students:
Creating a Campus Community of Care

Jesse J. Owen, Karen W. Tao,
and Emil R. Rodolfa

INTRODUCTION

College students' mental health concerns are becoming more severe than in past years (Gallagher, 2001; Benton, et al., 2003; Benton, et al., 2004). The recent advances in mental health care, along with more inclusive educational policies, have been associated with the increased numbers of students with chronic and acute mental health needs (NCASA, 2003). These changes in college and university students' mental health challenges have been met with a nationwide interest. For example, in 2005, the United States Congress passed the Campus Care Act, which provided federal funding to help campuses develop interventions for students with depression. In addition, various Web sites (i.e., Ulifeline, Collegeparents.org) offer college mental health resources and information to students and parents. These national efforts have been matched by increased campus responsiveness to meet the needs of a range of mental health issues and of the shifting demography of today's college students (Pace, Stamler, & Tarris, 1996; Jung, 2003; Perkins, Wesley, Haines, & Rice, 2005; Matusek, Wendt, & Wiseman, 2004; Zabinski, Celio, Jacobs, Manwaring, & Wilfey, 2003; Lee, Caruso, Goins, & Southerland, 2003; Yeater, Naugle, O'Donohue, & Bradley, 2004).

Notwithstanding the merits of such programs, most universities would benefit from comprehensive, campus-wide strategic practices for dealing with mental health issues. Accordingly, this chapter describes one approach to effectively intervene with *distressed and distressing students* whom we define as those students who are challenged by significant mental health concerns and whose impairment has the potential to negatively affect the larger college or university community. We describe a theoretical framework for developing and implementing a campus-wide strategic network to adequately provide prevention efforts for faculty, students, and families. The framework guides professionals in identifying, supporting, and intervening with distressed students.

THE CUBE MODEL: CAMPUS-WIDE STRATEGIC PLANNING FOR DISTRESSED & DISTRESSING STUDENTS

The cube model (Morrill, Oetting, & Hurst, 1974) provides a

theoretical framework that has been used extensively as a structure to promote the development of outreach programs and interdepartmental collaborations (Stone & Archer, 1990; Cooper, 2003). The cube model is comprised of three dimensions: (a) target of intervention (individual, primary group, associational group, and institution of community), (b) purpose of intervention (remediation, prevention, and development), and (c) method of intervention (direct service, consultation and training, and media) (Morrill, et al., 1974; Moore & Delworth, 1976).

As illustrated through the cube model, there are many avenues through which to assist distressed and distressing students. The essential mechanism is to develop a collaborative campus-wide strategic mental health plan that will create a safety net for students. The safety net can be conceptualized as a series of reciprocal relationships and feedback loops between campus units, such that the responsibility for the students' welfare is broadened to peers, faculty, staff, family members, and community leaders. This requires organized training for the members of the campus community (i.e., target of intervention) to identify and take action with distressed and distressing students. Furthermore, institutional-level interventions should have policies and procedures that allow a clear communication system for the various campus members and that protect the privacy of the students.

The cube model describes the purpose of interventions on three levels and creates a safety net for students that is primarily a remediation for distressed and distressing students. However, the program emphasizes prevention insofar as it assists students to get the help they need before things get worse (e.g., suicide, failing out of school). Moreover, the campus members will benefit from the training to help distressed and distressing students (i.e., purpose of intervention – development).

The method of intervention varies and includes psycho-educational programs, consultation, direct clinical service, and media. The intervention also varies as a function of resources, of the target of the intervention, and of its purpose. For example, faculty (i.e., target of intervention – associational group) can be identified to help distressed students within the department and act as a resource for students who may be unaware of mental health services. Moreover, the purpose of intervention for the college or university counseling center's staff is to offer preventive training programs (the method) to help faculty effectively address student concerns and to increase awareness of negative changes in student behavior or mood. Also, as inferred from this example, it is essential to have a collaborative approach that involves a diverse group of staff, faculty, and students in the planning process.

ESTABLISHING THE PLANNING TEAM FOR THE COLLABORATIVE CAMPUS-WIDE MENTAL HEALTH PLAN

There are a number of ways to conceptualize the development of a campus-wide network (e.g., top-down, bottom-up). We focus on a collaborative model and assume that the counseling center staff, given their status as the mental health experts on campus, will foster this mental health initiative. Ideally, the campus administration should provide support in the form of encouragement and tangible resources. Any attempts to develop a campus-wide collaborative network can easily be thwarted if support is not provided. Moreover, a representative from the administration should be present to increase communication between the planning team and the administration. Selection of the other members of the planning team will depend on the type and needs specific to the college or university. Generally included should be those departments that have a larger role in providing the interventions (i.e., counseling center, student judicial affairs, housing) and those that are targeted by the interventions (i.e., students, staff, and faculty).

This shift reflects the understanding that student mental health is not the sole responsibility of those with titles such as counselor, psychologist, or advisor.

The main task of the planning team would include a series of discussions that clarify the viability, pragmatism, and effectiveness of such a model. Planning and launching a campus-wide prevention program within a college or university system is an organizational challenge that will require open communication, patience, and persistence (Moore & Delworth, 1976; Coie, et al., 1993; Lewis, et al., 2003). The strength of a diverse collaborative planning team is that staff members in various campus departments have different training and philosophies and, as a result, will address the needs of students from different perspectives and different assessment and intervention models. For example, an academic advisor, although very much invested in a student's well-being, may be less focused on the symptoms of depression than on the student's ability to avoid academic probation and to remain in school. Accordingly, the intention of this collaborative approach is not to dilute the various roles, but to clarify them. In essence, members of each particular campus unit will use their training and expertise to best serve students. Collaboration and sharing of information, as is legally and ethically appropriate, results in a campus safety-net action plan. Essential units consequently know the relevant facts and are on the same page in developing a prevention and intervention plan for distressed and distressing students.

Furthermore, the planning team can use such resources as the

Jed Foundation's (2006) "Framework for Developing Institutional Protocols" to structure college or university policy and interventions. The Jed Foundation Framework provides guidelines and procedures to specifically address and respond to student concerns. This framework offers procedures to work with faculty and administrators associated with the student and to develop streamlined protocols for students who wish to re-enroll in school following a leave of absence.

GETTING STARTED: ASSESSMENT AND EVALUATION

The planning team begins by assessing the needs of the campus while simultaneously evaluating the effectiveness of current prevention and intervention efforts. Assessment should include regular reviews of students' mental health conditions and their severity, duration, and impact on academic and social functioning. Although most colleges and universities do not have the resources to conduct epidemiological research on student mental health, other approaches to assessing student functioning are available (e.g., surveys of student leaders, staff liaisons to student organizations and campus departments, student focus groups). Table 2.1 highlights some of the common student characteristics as well as campus environmental factors related to mental health issues. The planning team should review these personal and environmental factors to determine whether student needs can and are being met.

Figure 2.1: Individual and Environmental Influences.

The Self: Intra/Interpersonal Dynamics

Intrapersonal Dynamics	Interpersonal Dynamics
Personal expectations Mental health/substance abuse Self-esteem/identity/cultural factors	Ability to form relationships Academic performance Financial concerns Relationships w/peers and others Relationship w/family (expectations & environment) Cultural factors

The Environment

Campus Dynamics	Policies Governing the Campus
Safety issues Faculty/staff knowledge & response for mental health issues Collaboration with faculty/staff (network pragmatics) Course work (availability, difficulty of work, class size/assistance) Extracurricular possibilities & activities	Funding for resources Staff/faculty availability Policies for student health issues

In addition to student assessments, the team should evaluate the response capability of staff and faculty to ascertain the level of campus readiness. For example, some campuses may need to create a Crisis Response Team, which would involve individuals who are trained to manage and respond to student crises. Furthermore, the structures on campus should be evaluated to determine which specific student

needs are being met and which policies/procedures require modification. Because the individual and the environment are inextricably
linked, the college or university must ensure that students' needs can
be sufficiently accommodated. In addition, all campuses will benefit
from sharing with other campuses the results of their assessment and
program modification.

PREVENTION: CREATING THE SAFETY NET WITH FACULTY AND STUDENTS

The information acquired through assessment and from current
theories and research on prevention can enable counseling center staff
to deliver programs aimed at helping those who interact with students
on a regular basis. In the most recent American College Health Association Survey (2006), concerns about a friend were reported as one of
the top 10 causes for student academic interference. Almost 20% of
students indicated that during the past 12 months, they had become so
concerned about a friend that their academic coursework had suffered.
In addition, Sharkin and colleagues (2003) found that the majority of
college students spent some time attempting to help a friend in distress
(Sharkin, Plageman, Mangold, 2003).

Given these findings, students need knowledge of resources and
prevention strategies to assist their peers and themselves when confronted with distressing situations. Because students often report a
lack of knowledge about where to seek help, college and university
counseling center staff should inform students about campus resources
(e.g., free or low cost counseling services). For instance, in a survey
of Asian/Pacific Islander emerging leaders, Owen (2005) found that
approximately 50% of students were not aware of counseling services

on campus. One approach to increase student awareness is through psychoeducational programs. These programs serve the dual purpose of increasing the visibility of the counseling services and empowering students and faculty to help their peers/students.

Psychoeducational programs for students and faculty should be based on available research on risk and protective factors and should be focused on identification of key warning signs for common mental health problems (e.g., depression, anxiety, substance abuse, eating disorders, relationship issues). Moreover, these programs should offer tangible information for developing appropriate responses, destigmatizing mental health services, and maximizing the use of campus counseling services and other resources. This includes continuous education on how to establish professional and personal boundaries and on how to manage reactions to problems that distressed students may present. For example, at the University of California–Davis, the "Be A Friend" and "Distressed & Distressing Students: Faculty Concerns" programs educate students and faculty about how to help identify salient mental health warning signs and how to encourage students to seek professional help. Clearly, students and faculty/staff are in the best position to identify peers/students of concern and to encourage them to seek professional help.

The increased visibility of the counseling center and other campus resources is likely to create higher usage by students and their families. This increase should be recognized, a priori, and proper reinforcement should be provided, including the hiring of new staff and appropriate financial allocation commensurate with quantity of services provided.

CREATING THE SAFETY NET WITH FAMILIES

For many parents, their children's transition to college is unduly stressful. Nationally, there have been many discussions about the role parents should have in the welfare of their children during the college years. The notion that some parents are "hovering" or overly involved has received nationwide press, with such parents being referred to as "helicopter parents" (Shellenbarger, 2005). Furthermore, parent-based national organizations that enable parents to remain actively involved in and informed about their children's education (e.g., College Parents of America) are becoming more widely used. In addition, recent court decisions (e.g., Ewing I and Ewing II) have redefined the role that parents have in their children's (young adults') course of therapy. These legal decisions have put therapists on notice that they must take into account parental reports of dangerous behavior toward another individual, thus extending the requirements of the *Tarasoff* ruling. Although the courts have acknowledged a greater role for parents, the question remains: How involved *should* parents be in the mental health needs of their adult children? For instance, the Shin v. MIT case has highlighted the issue of parental notification.

Cases such as these raise questions about the legal and ethical limits of confidentiality for counseling centers and providers. If a distressed student seeks service at a college or university counseling center, should her parents be informed if the student is assessed to be a danger to self or others? Where is the ethical line, and how does counseling center staff respond to confidentiality and privileged communication dilemmas? Are there certain situations when a counseling staff member can inform parents and, if so, how should parents be contacted? How does a counseling center respond to concerned parents who call to inquire about their child? Ultimately, the dilemma posed is whether the privacy of the student supersedes the overall benefit of involving parents or guardians. A potential problem is that students might feel inhibited to express their concerns and problems with faculty, staff, and counseling center providers. Although there are no easy answers to these questions, they should be examined by the planning team in order to increase the effectiveness of responding to distressed and distressing students. At a minimum, campuses should develop informational resources (e.g., parent-student liaisons) and opportunities for parents to discuss concerns about their children's transition to campus. Orientations, focus groups, and Web sites may also be developed to offer ongoing information and support for parents needing further information on transition and other psychological issues.

CREATING THE SAFETY NET: THE ROLE OF THE COLLEGE OR UNIVERSITY DEAN OF STUDENTS

The dean of students, faculty, and staff are not bound by the confidentiality that mental health providers are required to uphold. Consequently, protocols should be established for the communication between them and the counseling center. For instance, when encountering a distressed or distressing student, faculty and staff should inform not only counseling center staff, but also consult with relevant department chairs and the dean of students.

The limits of confidentiality for counseling center staff have presented some difficulty, particularly when a student becomes a danger to him/herself or others. A few universities have, therefore, implemented policies that require a student to sign release of information forms. Thus counseling center staff members are allowed to inform the dean of students if a student is deemed to be danger to him/herself or others. However, these policies may have difficult ramifications for universities that take action based on a student's behavior. For example, a lawsuit (Allegheny v. Mahoney) was filed by a student who was expelled from school after expressing suicidal ideation. Universities should have clear policies regarding the exceptions to confidentiality when counseling is provided by college or university staff (e.g., university counseling center psychologist). Furthermore, if campus administrators require disclosures, they must clarify and be aware of whose needs they are prioritizing and the implications such decisions have on students' help-seeking attitudes and behavior.

MOVING FROM PREVENTION TO INTERVENTION: CODE OF CONDUCT AND MENTAL HEALTH

Excessive stress and multiple demands placed on students may sometimes result in a decreased ability to cope or function effectively. These difficulties in coping may often manifest themselves in maladaptive behaviors, which include disrupting a class, depending or placing stress on peers, or engaging in disorderly conduct on campus (Sharkin, et al., 2003). A college or university's response to such behavior is often based on the student's violation of codes of conduct rather than on possible mental health or personal causes of destructive behavior. For example, faculty or staff often immediately refer students exhibiting such behavior to the college or university judicial affairs board. To better assist distressed students, all concerned parties should collaborate to improve campus-wide response strategies and to provide a more comprehensive range of services for distressed students. However, the question then becomes: How much collaboration is in the best interest of students and the institution? Moreover, how should this collaborative intervention be coordinated?

INTERVENTION: COORDINATED SERVICES

Services for students should be coordinated carefully and thoughtfully. Crisis response teams comprised of faculty and staff members specifically concerned about a student's behavior may provide the best guidance to the campus when distressed students cause a disruption to the campus community.

Members of the crisis response team may include directors or designees from the following campus units:

(a) counseling center,

(b) student judicial affairs,

(c) disability services,

(d) campus counsel,

(e) college or university police,

(f) campus violence prevention program,

(g) dean of students,

(h) student health center director, and

(i) employee assistance program.

This broad-based group of individuals can respond to specific requests from faculty and staff, invite relevant campus community members to attend the meeting, and develop plans for the campus to follow when encountering distressed students. In essence, the members of a campus response team will create a needed safety net for both students and the larger campus community.

The response team should decide how best to communicate about the coordinated intervention for these distressed and distressing students. In general, there should be a protocol that enables campus units to communicate; however, the protocol can be challenging when some units (e.g., counseling services, judicial affairs) are bound by the legal requirements of confidentiality. Discussions of a student's problems and progress should be concise and focused on how to best ensure the student's safety and facilitate adequate functioning in the academic environment.

INTERVENTION: MEDICAL WITHDRAWAL

When is it considered best for a student to withdraw from classes? Universities should have clearly written policies about when to implement a mandatory student withdrawal for mental health or medical reasons. In most cases, responding to the student's misconduct (i.e., disruptive behavior) is preferred over withdrawing the student for medical reasons. However, if medical or mental health withdrawal is used, there should be explicit criteria that provide a clear pathway for a student's return to school.

INTERVENTION: COUNSELING CENTER

In addition to developing a collaborative team, counseling centers can intervene directly through psychoeducational programs (primary prevention), traditional treatment (secondary intervention), or crisis intervention (tertiary intervention). Primary prevention efforts can target both distressed and distressing students by teaching them to enhance their coping skills before problems develop (e.g., anticipate and prepare to cope effectively with stress and the rigors of academia). Primary prevention can also educate faculty and staff about how to identify and refer distressed students.

Counseling center staff members offer traditional counseling and psychotherapy interventions to help students increase their personal understanding and ability to cope in response to psychological problems and disorders. Due to increasing requests for clinical services, counseling center staff provides brief counseling services to students (i.e., 4 to 12 sessions). Brief counseling is common in most counseling centers (Stone & Archer, 1990), but longer-term therapy should be considered if it is necessary in light of the demands or disruptions made by students on campus. Although the provision of brief therapy is considered appropriate treatment for most problems presented by students, there are many benefits to providing longer-term therapy to distressed and distressing students within the counseling center. Frequently, students who are referred out do not follow through with the community referrals. As the number of students with intense and complex problems continues to increase, college and university clinicians and mental health providers will be compelled to offer these clients immediate stabilization, solution-focused, and/or symptom reduction techniques, rather than provide brief or short-term counseling.

Thus, it is also important to consider the role of the counseling center in providing more tertiary services, including crisis and on-call response interventions.

CONCLUSION

The changing demography of college and university campuses and the increasing number of students with severe mental health problems have placed counseling centers in a unique position. Counseling centers are not only central in the provision of student mental health services but are also fundamental in the coordination of campus response when services to emotionally distressed and distressing students are necessary. The cultivation of a campus community that can best meet the needs of diverse students requires clear, consistent, and ongoing communication between campus units, parents, and students. Ultimately, it is through a culture of collaboration that students' academic *and* personal well-being is ensured.

REFERENCES

Benton, S. A., Benton, S. L., Tseng, W. C., Newton, F. B., Benton, K. L., & Robertson, J. M. (2003). Changes in client problems: Contributions and limitations from a 13-year study. *Professional Psychology: Research and Practice, 34,* 66-72.

Benton, S. A., Benton, S. L., Newton, F. B., Benton, K. L., & Robertson, J. M. (2004). Changes in client problems: Contributions and limitations from a 13-year study. *Professional Psychology: Research and Practice, 35,* 317-319.

Chernoff, R. A., & Davison, G. C. (2005). An evaluation of a brief HIV/AIDS prevention intervention for college students using normative feedback and goal setting. *AIDS Education and Prevention, 17*(2), 91-104.

Coie, J. D., Watt, N. F., West, S. G., Hawkins, J. D., Asarnow, J. R., Markman, H. J., Ramey, S. L., Shure, M. B., & Long, B. (1993). The science of prevention: A conceptual framework and some directions for a national research program. *American Psychologist, 48,* 1013-1022.

Cooper, S. (2003). College counseling centers as internal organizational consultants to universities. *Consulting Psychology Journal: Practice and Research, 55*(4), 230-238.

Gallagher, R. P. (2001). *National survey of college counseling center directors 2001.* Washington, DC: International Association of Counseling Services.

The Jed Foundation. (2006). Framework for developing institutional protocols for the acutely distressed or suicidal college student. Retrieved June 6, 2006, from http://www.jedfoundation.org/framework.php

Lee, R. W., Caruso, M. E., Goins, S. E., & Southerland, J. P. (2003). *Journal of College Counseling, 6*(1), 14-24.

Lewis, V. A., Lewis, M. D., Daniels, J. A., & D'Andrea, M. J. (2003). *Community psychology: Empowerment strategies for a diverse society (3ʳᵈ ed.).* Pacific Grove, CA: Brooks/Cole.

Matusek, J. A., Wendt, S. J., & Wiseman, C.V. (2004). Dissonance thin-ideal and didactic healthy behavior eating disorder prevention programs: Results from a controlled trial. *International Journal of Eating Disorders, 36*(4), 376-388.

Morrill, W. H., Oetting, E. R., & Hurst, J. C. (1974). Dimensions of counselor functioning. *Personnel and Guidance Journal, 52,* 354-359.

Moore, M. & Delworth, U. (1976). *Training Manual for Student Service Program Development.* Boulder, CO: Western Interstate Commission for Higher Education.

Shellenbarger, S. (2005). Colleges ward off overinvolved parents. *The Wall Street Journal Online.* http://www.careerjournal.com/columnists/workfamily/20050729-workfamily.html?cjpartner=mktw

Stone, G. L., & Archer, J. (1990). College and university counseling centers in the 1990s: Challenges and limits. *The Counseling Psychologist, 18,* 539-607.

Wesley, P. H., Haines, M. P., & Rice, R. (2005). Misperceiving the college drinking norm and related problems: A nationwide study of exposure to prevention information, perceived norms and student alcohol misuse. *Journal of Studies on Alcohol, 66*(4), 470-478.

Yeater, E. A., Naugle, A. E., O'Donohue, W., & Bradley, A. R. Sexual assault prevention with college-aged women: A biblio-therapy approach. *Violence and Victims, 19*(5), 593-612.

Zabinski, M. F., Celi, A. A., Jacobs, J. M., Manwaring, J., & Wilfley, D. E. (2003). Internet-based prevention of eating disorder. *European Eating Disorders Review, 11*(3), 183-197.

CHAPTER 3

Legal Issues for Campus Administrators, Faculty, and Staff

Darby Dickerson

INTRODUCTION

Institutions of higher education are enrolling more students with mental health problems than ever before.[1] For many students, college is a period of transition and experimentation during which they face many challenges, some of which affect their mental well-being. These challenges often present colleges and universities with important legal and policy issues to resolve. Therefore, campus officials should strive to gain at least a rudimentary understanding of the most common legal issues that arise in the context of student mental health. Because these issues span a student's entire tenure, this chapter addresses legal issues associated with student mental health problems in the following contexts:

* admissions;

* accommodating admitted students with disabilities;

* confidentiality of student records;

* the campus alcohol culture;

* dangerous student behavior, including suicide;

* discipline and academic dismissal; and

* readmission.

This chapter is not intended to provide a comprehensive analysis of each issue addressed, or to provide legal advice about any particular situation. Instead, the chapter is designed to help campus officials realize when the law is implicated and when they should seek help from college or university counsel. An institution faced with a legal issue should always seek advice from a licensed attorney who can provide the institution with the most current law from the appropriate jurisdiction. That being said, in many situations, law alone will not completely answer the question presented. Instead, the answer must also be based on the school's educational mission, values, and policies, and the sound judgment of those trained in the particular issue at hand, whether that be a dean of student affairs, mental health counselor, or campus security officer.

For this reason, universities should consider adopting a philosophical vision of their relationship to students. This vision will help campus officials to better understand how law and policy relate to each other when resolving student issues. One such vision is the Facilitator Model, which was developed by Professors Peter F. Lake and Robert D. Bickel[2] and has been implemented with success at several institutions, including Arizona State, DePauw, Lynn, and Texas A&M Universities.

A Facilitator University understands that traditional college students are still developing mentally, physically, and emotionally; as such, they are neither children nor fully formed adults. Accordingly, the institution needs a special developmental perspective to promote a safe and sound educational environment. Under this perspective, the Facilitator University uses reasonable care to create conditions under which students will make responsible choices. In stark contrast to colleges and universities during the *in loco parentis* era, when the institution asserted autocratic control over its students, the Facilitator University does not presume to choose for students but empowers students to choose for themselves within a structured environment. As Bickel and Lake explain:

> Unlike parents, facilitators do not *choose* for students. Students must choose *for themselves* and shoulder significant responsibility for outcomes of their choice. The key is that the facilitator manages the parameters under which choices are made. Information, training, instruction and supervision, discussion, options, and, in some

cases, withdrawal of options are all appropriate for fa-
cilitators.[3]

In other words, a Facilitator University shares responsibility with
its students. Because students often make choices in an environment
that is largely beyond their control, the Facilitator University reasonably manages key factors to encourage better and safer student choices.
The Facilitator University also teaches students that they must act in
their own best interest, and in the best interest of others on campus.
This educational process involves the university connecting statements
of responsibility to statements of value and principle.

In a context that impacts mental health issues, students—due to
their relatively short tenure at a college or university—do not control
environmental factors such as the quality of residential halls and residential advising. Under the Facilitator Model, the college or university
would endeavor to provide satisfactory living arrangements for traditional college-aged students and would ensure that residential assistants (RAs) were properly screened, trained, and supervised. Among
other things, the institution would work to control physical conditions
that promote unhealthy behavior, such as trash in the halls, broken
locks and fixtures, and overcrowding. It would also work to re-train or
replace RAs who facilitate or ignore bad behavior, or who are not available during their designated hours. In addition, the institution would
enact policies and procedures to address these matters. For example,
it might include in the student handbook a policy regarding trash in
residential hallways and information about how to report broken locks.
It might also prepare and distribute to all students the institution's
expectations about the duties and responsibilities of RAs, and contact
information for full-time administrators who supervise the RAs. The

institution, however, must not stop with this step; it must also explain why cleanliness, working locks, and diligent RAs are important to students' health and safety. For instance, the institution might explain that if an RA is not available during posted hours, and an emergency occurs, valuable time—and possibly lives—might be lost. The institution might also educate students that RAs are not hired primarily to find and report bad behavior, but to promote safety in the residence halls. The institution might share a concrete example in which the RA contacts emergency medical technicians when a student passes out from excessive alcohol use, or contacts campus counselors or the dean of students if a student believes her roommate is severely depressed or suicidal. By tying values and principles to rules—and by adding concrete examples—students will be more likely to make wiser choices in their day-to-day lives.

Adopting the Facilitator Model will affect choices the institution makes concerning legal issues. For example, the Facilitator University will aspire to be proactive, not reactive. In this regard, it will create collaborative risk-management teams that will identify risks, evaluate and implement solutions, and train members of the campus community to act in ways that promote health and safety and also avoid or minimize physical and legal risks. It will train administrators to use reasonable care to promote student safety. A Facilitator University will (a) provide professional administrators with the room to exercise sound discretion without fearing legal consequences; (b) use the law to empower campus officials to create a safer campus; and (c) implement policies and procedures that share responsibility with students and that educate students about the values and principles underlying those policies. A Facilitator University understands that it should not fear "creating duties," as those duties are likely to exist already, and instead should focus on acting reasonably and providing students with an environment within which they can make responsible choices. A Facilitator University will engage legal counsel in the decision-making process but will make a safe educational environment—not the avoidance of legal liability—the top priority.

ADMISSIONS

Campus officials and faculty who serve on admissions commit-tees must be sensitive to legal issues relating to applicants with men-tal health disabilities. Section 504 of the Rehabilitation Act of 1973 (Section 504)[4] and the Americans with Disabilities Act of 1990 (ADA)[5] both prohibit discrimination against individuals with disabilities, including mental disabilities. Many states and municipalities also have nondiscrimination laws, and universities should consult those laws when reviewing their admissions processes and practices.

SECTION 504 OF THE REHABILITATION ACT

Section 504 prohibits universities that receive federal funding from discriminating against individuals with disabilities (29 U.S.C. § 794(a); 34 C.F.R. § 104.41 [2006]).[6] As a practical matter, virtually all institutions of higher education receive some sort of federal funding, and are thus subject to Section 504.

The federal regulations that implement Section 504 provide that institutions of higher education may not discriminate against qualified, but handicapped, applicants in the recruitment or admissions process-es. A handicapped individual is one who has a mental or physical im-pairment that substantially limits a major life activity, "has a record of such . . . impairment," "or is regarded as having such an impairment" (34 C.F.R. § 104.3(j)(1)).[7] "Mental impairment" means "any mental or psychological disorder, such as mental retardation, organic brain syndrome, emotional or mental illness, and specific learning disabilities" (34 C.F.R. § 104.3(j)(2)(ii)).[8] An applicant with a mental impairment is "qualified" if he or she "meets the academic and technical standards essential for admission to, or participation in, the . . . educational program" (34 C.F.R. § 104.3(l)(3)).[9]

During the admissions process, institutions of higher education are prohibited from limiting the number or proportion of handicapped students who may be admitted, and are generally prohibited from using admissions tests and criteria that have "a disproportionate, adverse effect on handicapped persons or any class of handicapped persons." Institutions of higher education must also ensure that admissions tests are selected and administered in ways that reflect the aptitude and achievement of individuals with disabilities (34 C.F.R. § 104.42(b)(2)–(3)).[10] Rulings by the Office of Civil Rights (OCR), however, indicate that most widely accepted tests and measures may be used in the admissions process, even when the applicant has a disability. For example, a law school may use the LSAT (law school admissions test) as an admissions requirement,[11] universities may deny admission to a candidate with a mental impairment whose GRE (graduate record examinations) score fell below that of all other accepted applicants,[12] and a university may reject an applicant with a psychiatric disability if he or she was not in academic good standing at a previous school,[13] or if accommodating the student would require the institution to waive its minimum admissions standards.[14]

On an admissions application, a college or university generally may not ask whether the candidate has a disability (34 C.F.R. §§

104.6(b), 104.42(b)(4), 104.42(c)).[15] It may include those questions, however, if it is taking remedial action to correct the effects of past discrimination against disabled individuals, or to overcome past conditions that resulted in limited participation by individuals with disabilities.[16] If a school makes such a pre-admissions inquiry, the application must clearly state that the information is sought for a remedial purpose, the applicant has the option to provide the information, the information will be kept confidential, and refusal to provide the information will not subject the applicant to adverse treatment (34 C.F.R. § 104.42(c)).[17]

The OCR also has carved out other limited exceptions to the prohibition on pre-admissions inquiries about disabilities. First, the OCR has determined that if an institution has reasonable concerns about the safety of a potential student and others on campus, it may deny admission or require the applicant to provide additional information about the disability and its impact. For example, the OCR held that the Community College of Southern Nevada could deny admission to an applicant who, during an interview, stated that he often thought about killing people.[18] In a similar situation, however, the OCR held that the school must consider the applicant's actual history, as opposed to solely considering the nature of the disability. In that case, which involved Penn State University, an applicant diagnosed as a paranoid schizophrenic behaved in a disruptive manner during his pre-admissions meetings with campus officials. As a result, the college asked the applicant to release information from psychiatrists and other references. This request was made in connection with a college policy designed to protect the campus from dangerous persons. The OCR determined that the policy, as administered, violated Section 504 because it did not distinguish between disabled applicants who posed a substantial risk of harm and those who merely had a history of a certain disability.[19]

Second, a college or university can ask an applicant to provide information about criminal activity, even if the activity relates to a disability.[20] Finally, in certain special programs where the well-being of others is at stake, such as the priesthood or a post-graduate counseling program, a school may request the results of psychological examinations as part of the admissions process.[21] The last exception, however, will not apply in most academic programs.[22]

AMERICANS WITH DISABILITIES ACT

The ADA was based in large measure on Section 504, and the two statutes impose virtually the same requirements on institutions of higher education.[23] Title II of the ADA prohibits discrimination in access to services and programs provided by public entities, such as public colleges and universities, and Title III prohibits discrimination in access to places of public accommodation, such as private colleges and universities.[24] The ADA and its related regulations[25] do not affect an institution's obligations under Section 504.[26]

As with Section 504, the ADA prohibits discrimination against otherwise qualified individuals with disabilities. A qualified applicant is one "who with or without reasonable modifications to rules, policies, or practices . . . meets the essential eligibility requirements" to participate in the program.[27] "Disability" includes a mental impairment that substantially limits a major life activity.[28] The corresponding regulations clarify that "mental impairment" includes mental retardation, organic brain syndrome, emotional or mental illness, and specific learning disabilities. The term does not include transvestism, transsexualism, pedophilia, exhibitionism, voyeurism, gender identity disorders not resulting from physical impairments, or other sexual behavior disorders; compulsive gambling, kleptomania, or pyromania; or psychoactive substance use disorders resulting from current illegal use of drugs.[29] A mental impairment also does not include personality traits such as irritability, stress, poor judgment or impulse control, personality conflicts, panic disorder, bizarre behavior, or irresponsible behavior.[30] Drug addiction is listed in the statute and regulations as a disability, but impairments from or conditions caused by current drug use are excepted.[31]

As under Section 504, schools may not impose or apply eligibility criteria that actually, or tend to, screen out individuals with disabilities, except in limited circumstances.[32] This means that universities in their admissions-related tests and activities must reasonably accommodate the needs of disabled applicants.[33]

COLLEGE AND UNIVERSITY ADMISSIONS PROCESSES

Colleges and universities should consider the steps listed below to help ensure that institutional goals of diversity and access are furthered within the controlling legal environment.

First, campus officials should review the school's admissions policies and nondiscrimination policy against Section 504, the ADA, and local nondiscrimination laws that might provide applicants with even broader protection. These policies should be reviewed and updated regularly to keep pace with new legal developments.

The college or university should include its nondiscrimination policy on admissions materials, including the admissions application.

It also should explain how the nondiscrimination policy relates to the school's mission and values.

The college or university must not limit the number or proportion of students with mental disabilities who may be accepted into a school, class, or particular department or major. Colleges and universities should also study whether their eligibility requirements tend to screen out applicants with disabilities. If so, the college or university should examine whether alternatives might be available that have a lesser impact but achieve the same result in terms of appropriately determining qualifications.

The college or university should avoid pre-admission inquiries—on the application or otherwise—about whether the applicant has a mental disability, unless the inquiry falls into one of the narrow, remedial exceptions. If a college or university invites self-identification of a disability as part of a special admissions process, it must ensure that the application and other admissions material clearly explain how the process works, advise the applicant that disclosure of a disability is voluntary, provide that the disclosure will remain confidential, and indicate that an applicant will not be penalized for refusing to provide the optional information.

With regard to the actual application form, the college or university should remove questions that ask whether a standardized test required for admission was taken under non-standard time limits. On a related point, the college or university should inform applicants, on the Web and in admissions brochures, about how to request accommodations for admissions tests. In most instances, the college or university also should eliminate questions about an applicant's treatment for mental health or emotional problems.

Admissions officers should segregate voluntary disclosures[34] of disabilities from other admissions materials and place that information in a separate, secure location where it can later be forwarded to the disabilities services office if so requested by an admitted applicant. Self-disclosures can arise in a variety of ways. A recent survey found that 61% of applicants with a disability disclose it during the admissions process. Self-disclosure can occur on the application form, in the personal essay, in letters of recommendation, during the personal interview, and in other communications. Admissions officers also should segregate medical records from the rest of a student's admissions file.

Experienced admissions professionals, along with legal counsel, should train faculty, staff, and others involved with the admissions process—such as alumni recruiters and interviewers—about how to work with disabled applicants. In addition, universities are required to implement and publicize a process to handle disputes about disabilities that might arise during the applications process.[35]

In addition to the steps noted above, a Facilitator University would focus on fulfilling the institution's educational mission and promoting a safe campus environment. This might be accomplished by implementing a policy on background checks for applicants. Although it might not yet be feasible to conduct complete checks on all students, universities could draw on the expertise of their campus security department, admissions officers, judicial conduct officials, and senior student affairs leadership to develop a list of "red flags" that would, should they appear in an applicant's files, trigger a more rigorous review. Examples include past violence, dishonorable military discharge, patterns of illegal drug use or DUIs, loss of a professional license, unexplained time gaps after high school, or dismissal from another college or university.

Not all students with mental disabilities are good candidates for higher education or residential higher education. The Facilitator University understands this distinction and would not allow fear of legal action to prevent it exercising its best judgment in the admissions process. If, based on an individualized review of past conduct and the expertise of institution professionals, an applicant presents a threat, that applicant should not be admitted.[36]

A Facilitator University would also expressly connect the benefits and strengths of a heterogeneous student body to rules regarding consideration of disabilities in the admissions process. It would create an environment in which qualified but disabled students are not merely tolerated but are a welcome and meaningful part of the community. This might be accomplished through disability awareness programs for faculty, staff, and students, by encouraging students with disabilities to seek leadership opportunities on campus, and by working with qualified professionals to create ways for students to showcase their special abilities. The Facilitator University recognizes that a positive campus environment will help attract talented, high-caliber students of all sorts, including ones with disabilities or special abilities.

ACCOMMODATING ADMITTED STUDENTS WITH MENTAL, EMOTIONAL, AND PSYCHIATRIC DISABILITIES

Once a student with a disability is admitted, the institution may have a duty to provide reasonable accommodations.[37] As in the admissions context, the two primary federal statutes that control are Section 504 of the Rehabilitation Act of 1973 and the Americans with Disabilities Act of 1990.

In the student setting, a reasonable accommodation is a modification or adjustment that will allow a qualified but disabled individual to participate on a level playing field and to take advantage of programs and services offered by the college or university.[38] However, schools are not required to fundamentally alter the nature of the program[39] and need not grant accommodations that impose an undue resource burden or a direct threat to health or safety.[40] In determining whether an undue burden exists, the college or university should consider the nature and cost of the requested accommodation in light of the institution's overall financial resources.[41] A "direct threat" refers to a significant risk to health or safety that cannot be eliminated by reasonable accommodation.[42] For example, in *Ascani v. Hofstra University* (1999),[43] the court held that the university need not accommodate a student with a mental disability by providing an academic advisor or counseling services when the student harassed and threatened a professor. Thus, as a practical matter, the law regarding reasonable accommodations allows a college or university to determine, post-admission, that an individual's disability renders him or her unqualified to participate in the academic program.[44]

A college or university is required to provide reasonable accommodations only after the student discloses and sufficiently validates a recognized disability that affects a major life activity and requests accommodations.[45] An institution of higher education does not violate Section 504 or the ADA by refusing to provide accommodations when the student fails to provide the required notification or documentation.[46] When an accommodation is granted, it must relate to the disability.[47] In addition, the college or university need not accept a disabled student's request for a specific accommodation if it provides a reasonable alternative.[48] Moreover, when an accommodation involves academic matters, courts typically respect the faculty's professional judgment.[49]

Reasonable accommodations that a school provides to a student with mental, emotional, or psychiatric disabilities can vary widely, depending on the type and severity of the condition. Indeed, the law requires that accommodations be individualized.[50] A human factor that campus officials should keep in mind is that students with "hidden disabilities" "often feel a stigma associated with their disabilities and believe faculty and other students do not understand their need for accommodations."[51]

Remembering that accommodations must be individuated and that universities need not fundamentally alter their academic programs, some types of accommodations that might be considered for students with mental, emotional, or psychiatric disabilities include the following:[52]

* extending the time to complete a course or the program;

* granting a course substitution;

* reducing the student's course load in one or more semesters;

* granting additional time to complete examinations;

* allowing a student to dictate examination answers;

* providing a quiet testing area;

❉ providing a note-taker, reader, or software that reads aloud;

❉ granting permission for the student to record classes, or making recordings of classes available;

❉ assigning the student a specific seat in a classroom; and

❉ assigning the student a single-occupancy residence hall room.

When reviewing requests for accommodation, the best practice is to rely on the professional documentation provided by the student or obtained by the institution.[53] In addition, administrators who review and grant accommodations should discuss classroom- and course-related accommodations with the professors, as they will have the best knowledge about course requirements and assessment. For example, if an administrator grants a disabled student double time on examinations, but does not realize that the professor administers pop-quizzes on a regular basis, problems are likely to arise. Once the accommodations are finalized and granted, the administrator should inform affected professors about accommodations that will impact classroom and course administration,[54] and should also remind the professors to keep the accommodations confidential.[55]

Below are steps campus officials might consider taking to assure that students entitled to reasonable accommodations receive them.

❀ Ensure the institution's disability policies are current, consistent with federal, state, and local law, and are publicized to applicants and students.

❀ Develop a statement about who is a qualified applicant for a particular academic program by articulating the critical functions that a student in the program must perform.

❀ Develop a consistent, detailed policy for documentation by consulting the "Guidelines for Documentation of Psychiatric Disabilities in Adolescents and Adults," prepared by the Educational Testing Service Network.[56]

❀ Implement a deliberative process to handle requests for accommodation. This process should show that the college or university exercises reasonable, professional judgment when considering requests for accommodation and formulates individualized accommodations that relate to the student's disability.

❀ If possible, delegate the issue of accommodations to a trained disability expert, who will then work with others, such as academic deans, faculty members, and other administrators.[57]

❀ Identify a disabilities grievance officer and develop a sound disabilities grievance process.

In addition to these steps, a Facilitator University would strive to provide counseling services to help teach disabled students about their rights and responsibilities and about the institution's rights and responsibilities. It would develop disability awareness programs and would explain to the campus community why providing reasonable accommodations furthers the institution's mission and values and creates a level playing field, not an advantage. In addition, the Facilitator University would strive to create an environment in which individuals with disabilities were accepted into the community and valued for their contributions.

CONFIDENTIALITY

Properly preserving the confidentiality of certain student information is an important responsibility for institutions of higher education. Although many types of laws impact student privacy, this section will briefly address three: the Family Education Rights and Privacy Act of 1974 (FERPA, also known as the Buckley Amendment),[58] the Health Insurance Portability and Accountability Act of 1996 (HIPAA),[59] and state statutes that protect confidentiality of certain counseling and mental health records. This section will also touch on the ethical obligations that certain licensed professionals have to students they treat.

FERPA

FERPA is a federal law that protects the privacy of student educational records.[60] FERPA applies to all schools that receive funds through an applicable program of the U.S. Department of Education;[61] for this reason, the law covers most institutions of higher education. If a student is enrolled in a postsecondary institution of higher education, the student holds the FERPA rights, even if he or she is under 18.[62]

FERPA pertains to a student's "education records." Schools may disclose the contents of educational records only when the student consents, when the disclosure meets a statutory exemption, or when the disclosure concerns directory information, such as name and address, and the student has not opted out.[63]

Although FERPA's definition of educational records includes most health information, it expressly *excludes* student medical records that:

1. pertain to students who are 18 years of age or older, or who are attending an institution of postsecondary education;

2. are made or maintained by a physician, psychiatrist, psychologist, or other recognized professional or para-professional serving or assisting in that capacity;

3. are made, maintained, or used only in connection with providing treatment to a student; and

4. are not available to anyone other than the persons providing such treatment, except as a physician or other appropriate professional of the student's choice.[64]

Once shared, however, the records become educational records subject to FERPA.[65]

A college or university may, without a student's consent, disclose

educational records to the following persons, in the following circumstances:[66]

* to other school officials, including faculty, whom the
  institution has determined have "legitimate educational interests;"

* to officials at another institution of higher education
  "where the student seeks or intends to enroll;"

* "in connection with a health or safety emergency,"
  "if knowledge of the information is necessary to
  protect the health or safety of the student or other
  individuals;"[67]

* in connection with a disciplinary proceeding at the institution;[68] and

* to the parent of a student under 21 if the student violates any federal, state, or local law, or any institution
  policy concerning alcohol or other drugs that result in
  a disciplinary violation.

Certain records also may be disclosed to a victim of a crime of
violence or a non-forcible sex offense.[69]

With regard to issues of health and safety, FERPA *does not* prevent
a college or university from taking the following actions:

❧ including in a student's education records appropriate information concerning disciplinary action taken against the student for conduct that posed a significant risk to the safety or well-being of that student, other students, or other members of the school community;

❧ disclosing appropriate information to teachers and campus officials who have a legitimate educational interest in the student's behavior; or

❧ sharing appropriate information with teachers and campus officials at other schools who have a legitimate educational interest in the student's behavior.[70]

It is important to remember that FERPA applies to the disclosure of *tangible records* and to information derived from tangible records. It does not protect the confidentiality of information in general, and does not protect information obtained through personal knowledge or observation.[71]

With these exceptions to disclosure, universities have sufficient latitude to respond to situations that relate to, or may be created by, students with mental health challenges. For example, if a campus official determines that a student is in crisis, that official may contact the student's family, or other individuals, such as doctors or counselors, who might assist with the situation. If a student has a condition about which certain professors or staff should know, FERPA also permits that information to be disclosed.

FERPA does not provide a student with a private right of action against an institution of higher education.[72] Accordingly, when a campus official believes that disclosure is required to protect a student, to respond to an emergency, or to maintain health and safety on campus, he or she can make that decision without worrying about subjecting the institution to significant legal exposure. That is not to say that other consequences might not attach to an improper disclosure under FERPA. For example, a disclosure permitted under the health and safety exception to FERPA might result in defamation liability if made in an overly broad fashion beyond those with a legitimate need to know. However, it is always important for campus officials to weigh all factors involved. For instance, most universities, including Facilitator Universities, would risk a FERPA inquiry from the Department of Education to protect students and other members of the community from death or serious injury.

HIPAA

Although an expert understanding of the Health Insurance Portability and Accountability Act of 1996 (HIPAA) requires wading through mounds of bureaucratic regulations,[73] at its core, HIPAA governs the use and disclosure of private health information.[74] "Health information" is broadly defined, and includes any information, in any format, that:

1. is created or received by a health care provider, health plan, public health authority, employer, life insurer, school, or health care clearinghouse; and

2. relates to the past, present, or future physical or mental health or condition of an individual; the provision of health care to an individual; or the past, present, or

future payment for the provision of health care to an individual.[75]

HIPAA's privacy regulations apply to three types of entities: health plans, health care clearinghouses, and health care providers that transmit health information in electronic form in connection with certain financial and administrative transactions.[76] Covered transactions include the electronic transmission of information in connection with billing, health plan eligibility, and health plan enrollment and disenrollment.[77]

Universities may be subject to HIPAA regulations if they offer health-care services in departments, units, or schools whose staff make electronic transactions.[78] However, if a college or university clinic provides health services but does not engage in electronic transactions, then the privacy regulations do not apply. Posting to a student's online account a bill from a student health center that will be paid by the student or his or her parent is not a standard electronic transaction with a third-party payor, and is thus not covered under HIPAA.[79]

It is also significant that information a student health center creates, receives, or maintains with respect to students typically is not considered protected health information and is thus not subject to HIPAA. Education records covered by FERPA and those student medical records excluded by FERPA are not considered to be protected health information. Interestingly, no records are covered by both HIPAA and FERPA. Thus, student medical records are technically exempt from both FERPA and HIPAA. Essentially, this means that universities may continue to treat their student records as they traditionally have in accordance with FERPA and state law.

State Statutes

Some states have enacted legislation that concerns the confidentiality of counseling and other mental health treatment records. For example, Section 19-11-95 of the South Carolina Code protects the confidences of patients with mental illness or emotional conditions. Under this statute, a licensed mental health provider should not reveal client confidences except in limited circumstances. Permitted disclosures include those allowed by other statutes or laws and when the patient intends to commit a crime or harm himself. A required exception exists when disclosure is required by statutory law or by court order, to the extent that the patient's care and treatment, or the nature and extent of his mental illness or emotional condition are reasonably at issue. Other states have similar statutes.

Ethical Obligations

Physicians, psychiatrists, and other licensed mental health professionals are bound by ethics codes that, under most circumstances, prevent them from revealing client confidences to others. Universities must understand the ethical obligations of these employees and how the ethics codes interact with state laws, which often vary in terms of scope of coverage and permissible or required disclosures. The conflict between maintaining confidentiality in student counseling and working with faculty and staff on matters of student behavior and discipline has always been complicated.

During summer 2006, officials at The George Washington University contemplated requiring students seeking help at the university counseling center to sign a waiver that would have allowed information discussed with mental health professionals to be shared with administrators, without limit. At most college and university counseling centers, students are assured of confidentiality unless they reveal information that suggests that they may harm themselves or others. Ultimately, the university decided not to implement the new policy. Although the university did not provide the specific bases for its decision, opponents of the policy argued that it would have conflicted with the professional ethical standards and discouraged students from seeking treatment for fear of stigma or disclosure.[80]

To effectively manage confidentiality issues, the college or university should, among other steps, engage legal counsel to review pertinent laws and ethical codes, train affected staff, and include clear and honest statements about the limits of confidentiality in informed-consent documens provided to student-patients.[81]

CONSIDERATIONS FOR STRIKING A BALANCE BETWEEN PRESERVING CONFIDENTIALITY AND PROMOTING CAMPUS SAFETY

To protect student privacy at an appropriate level while protecting campus safety, college or university officials should consider taking the following steps:

* Review internal policies and procedures to make sure they comport with state and federal privacy laws.

* Ensure that faculty and key campus officials understand pertinent privacy laws and internal policies that also might protect confidential student information.

❉ Provide training so that the campus community understands that overall health and safety concerns will almost always trump privacy rules.

❉ Educate students about what is and is not private, and under what circumstances private information may be released.

❉ Understand that some campus employees, such as licensed counselors, psychiatrists, psychologists, and physicians often are subject to higher levels of confidentiality under the law and under professional ethical standards.

❉ Determine whether the institution is covered by HIPAA and work with an attorney familiar with HIPAA to develop appropriate protocols, especially in connection with clinics, health facilities, and medical centers.

Under the Facilitator Model, the college or university would seek to balance privacy concerns against the health and safety of students and the campus in general. Although it is usually possible to protect health and safety within the confines of controlling law, fears of technical legal breaches should not paralyze campus officials from taking steps that will prevent injury or death. In addition, a Facilitator University would develop ways to encourage students to permit disclosures to advance their own growth and development, and to help protect their own well-being and the well-being of those around them.

ALCOHOL

Many students with mental health issues self-medicate with alcohol and other drugs.[82] On the flip side, alcohol and other drugs can themselves trigger mental health issues. It is not an understatement to say that alcohol is the linchpin of virtually all negative student conduct on campuses. Accordingly, alcohol and other drug prevention is paramount in the context of responding to student mental health issues on campus.

In the 1970s and 1980s, courts typically protected universities in cases involving student injuries that resulted from alcohol consumption. These courts found that college students were adults capable of making their own decisions on non-academic matters, that alcohol use by students was uncontrollable, and that alcohol-prevention efforts were thus not effective, and that college is a rite of passage and drinking is a part of that journey.[83]

TRENDS

More recently, however, courts started taking a different view of universities' relationships to their students, and universities' liability in alcohol-related cases. As explained by Peter Lake and Joel Epstein, the trend is toward "notions of (a) shared responsibility for alcohol risks in college culture and (b) responsibility to create a more responsible alcohol culture."[84] Moreover, recognizing that the assumptions of the 1970s and 1980s were incorrect and that alcohol culture can be effectively managed through various science-based approaches, campus officials should assume that courts in the future may expect universities to use science-based programs to address high-risk alcohol and other drug use.

A brief sampling of cases that reflect this shift includes:

❀ *Furek v. University of Delaware* (1991), in which the University of Delaware was held liable for a serious alcohol-related hazing injury that occurred during an on-campus fraternity event;[85]

❀ *Knoll v. Board of Regents of the University of Nebraska* (1999), in which the Nebraska Supreme Court ruled that universities have a shared duty to prevent alcohol-related hazing injuries, even when those injuries occurred in a fraternity's off-campus, non-university-owned premise;[86]

❀ *Coghlan v. Beta Theta Pi Fraternity* (1999), in which the University of Idaho was held responsible for preventing dangers associated with high-risk alcohol use by an underage freshman participating in rush;[87] and

❀ *McClure v. Fairfield University* (2003), in which the court denied the university's motion for summary judgment against a student who, as a pedestrian, had been injured off campus by a drunken student returning from private parties at the beach, and indicated that, under the circumstances, the University "had a duty to protect students who traveled to and from parties at the beach area."[88]

McClure is significant because it discusses the legal drinking age in

Connecticut, high-risk alcohol use among college students, the school's anti-alcohol policy, its failure to attempt to enforce that policy at the beach parties, and the school's safe-ride program. Arguably, this discussion reflects the court's expectation that universities will acknowledge the issue of high-risk alcohol use on campus and design and implement effective policies and programs to more effectively manage the campus alcohol culture.[89]

In response to the changing legal and policy environment, many colleges and universities have found the science-based environmental management approach to be an effective method to combat high-risk alcohol use.[90] Environmental management has its roots in public heath, and, as its name implies, is designed to change the campus environment. "Environmental management means moving beyond general awareness and other education programs to identify and change those factors in the physical, social, legal, and economic environment that promote or abet" the specific problem.[91] Universities that adopt the environmental management approach combat high-risk alcohol and drug use by coordinating the efforts of all major functionaries—both on and off campus—who are impacted by, or who can impact, students' alcohol use.

Successful environmental management programs depend heavily upon strong collaboration across campus and between the campus and the greater community. In the context of alcohol and other drug prevention, colleges and universities have learned that it does take a village to make a difference; everyone on campus has to perceive that they play a role in prevention. The best programs are campus-wide efforts that involve faculty, a wide variety of staff, students, alumni, parents, and others.[92] These programs are multi-pronged, environmental, and often include:

❀ general awareness and other educational programs;

❀ awareness weeks and peer-education programs;

❀ "curriculum infusion," in which professors incorporate alcohol- and drug-related lessons into their courses;

❀ social norms campaigns, which, among other things, seek to provide "more accurate information about actual levels of alcohol use on campus;"

❀ harm-reduction programs, such as safe-ride programs;

❀ alcohol-free events;

❀ social and recreational options during the late night and early morning hours when the alcohol culture is most active;

❀ scheduling Friday morning classes and encouraging faculty to give quizzes and set assignment deadlines on Thursdays and Fridays;

❀ programs to identify and refer to intervention services students who have problems with alcohol and drug use;

❧ collaborative on-campus teams that share information, recommend new solutions, and evaluate the effectiveness of various programs;

❧ campus-community coalitions that helped to change the off-campus environment; for example, some coalitions have worked with tavern owners to enforce existing laws and to encourage the owners not to hold events, such as low-price promotions, that encourage high-risk drinking; and

❧ efforts to tighten statewide alcohol regulations and to change alcohol laws.[93]

Environmental management approaches are favored by the U.S. Department of Education-sponsored Higher Education Center,[94] and the concept of environmental management has been endorsed by major scientific reports, including the National Academy of Sciences and Institute of Medicine's 2003 report titled "Reducing Underage Drinking—A Collective Responsibility,"[95] and the National Institute on Alcoholism and Alcohol Abuse's 2002 reports on the campus alcohol culture.[96] The environmental management approach is also consistent with the Facilitator Model in that it promotes shared responsibility for student safety, the university's use of reasonable care, and university management of key environmental factors, such as residence halls, that can enhance responsible student choices.

College and University Response to the Campus Alcohol Culture

Although more policy than law-oriented, universities should seriously consider implementing an environmental management plan, which might include using the Core Alcohol and Drug Survey[97] to determine the extent of high-risk drinking on campus, collaborative risk-management teams to identify risks and solutions to the campus alcohol culture,[98] campus-community coalitions to involve the greater community in the fight against high-risk drinking, longitudinal social norming campaigns to help students understand actual statistics about drinking among peers, and various educational and programming options that would help invade the time and space currently consumed by the alcohol culture, which tends to thrive between midnight and dawn.[99]

In addition, universities should educate students and key campus officials about their state's legal environment regarding alcohol. It is important, for example, to understand minimum drinking ages, dram-shop acts, laws concerning social-host liability, and whether and when establishments such as bars and restaurants are prohibited from serving visibly intoxicated patrons.

Finally, it is important for the college or university to explain to students, in their handbooks and other publications, the institution's policies about alcohol use. These policies, however, should go beyond merely stating the "may's" and "don'ts." Instead, to help students make the best decisions possible about their own health and safety, they should also explain the "why's" underlying those policies and should connect statements of responsibility to statements of value and principle. For example, the institution might explain that alcohol use has been linked to the frequency of accidents, injuries, date and acquaintance rape, sexual misconduct, sexually transmitted diseases, violence, drug use, financial irresponsibility, poor academic performance, and attrition. The institution might also note that students who frequently participate in high-risk drinking are significantly more likely than other students to be hurt or injured, hurt or injure others, drive a car after drinking, get into trouble with law enforcement, engage in unplanned and unprotected sex, damage property, fall behind in class work, and miss class. They might also include information reflecting the strong correlation between alcohol use and eating disorders, depression, suicide, and other mental health issues.[100] In other words, in this age of shared responsibility for student safety, universities should provide students with information to make the best choices for their own safety under the circumstances.[101]

DANGEROUS STUDENT BEHAVIOR

Institutions long have been concerned about students whose conduct poses a danger to themselves or to others. When thinking about the dangers that students may pose, it is important to note that students whose seeming intent is to hurt themselves—such as students who are suicidal—may also pose a danger to others. For example, if the student chooses to kill herself by using fire or fumes, she may injure or kill others in the vicinity. In addition, "suicidal ideation is a continuum and can be linked to unintentional injury and homicide."[102]

STUDENTS WHO POSE A DANGER TO THEMSELVES

Students who pose a danger to themselves include students who exhibit suicidal ideation and other self-destructive conduct, such as cutting and eating disorders.[103] In these situations, various questions arise regarding both the student's and the institution's rights and responsibilities. Although the discussion below focuses on student suicide, the lessons and principles can be applied to other instances of self-destructive behavior.

STUDENT SUICIDE

Approximately 1,100 college students die each year by suicide.[104] Suicide is also the second leading cause of death among college students and the third leading cause within the 15–24 age group.[105] As such, it is estimated that "[m]ore teenagers and young adults die from suicide than from all medical illnesses combined."[106] The Jed Foundation has found that most college-aged students who committed suicide were not in treatment with a mental health professional at the time of their death, even though approximately 90% of individuals who commit suicide have a diagnosable mental illness, most often depression.[107] As with alcohol abuse, suicide is a public health, or environmental, issue that requires the attention and resources of the entire campus community.[108]

As explained by Peter Lake and Nancy Tribbensee in their leading article on legal issues related to college-student suicide, "[t]he American legal system has been reluctant to hold institutions liable for suicide or self-inflicted injury. Traditionally, an individual who committed suicide was thought to be the sole 'proximate cause' of injury; therefore, other entities were not responsible for the suicide."[109] More recently, two exceptions to the general rule have emerged. Liability has been found when the defendant was determined to have caused the suicide and when the defendant was determined to have a duty to prevent the suicide.[110] Under each exception, courts rejected the traditional no-proximate-causation rule and found that the suicide was foreseeable.[111] "Suicide is no longer an intervening act that cuts off the chain of liability. Therefore, a defendant who falls within either of these two exceptions may be subject to liability for the resulting suicide."[112]

Under the first exception, a defendant who illegally or improperly provides liquor or illegal substances can be liable for a resulting suicide.[113] Lake and Tribbensee indicate that "[c]olleges and universities also must contend with the potential liability for suicide if the university wrongly and maliciously accuses a student under an honor or disciplinary code, if the student is subjected to severe physical hazing that may lead to suicide, or if the student is subjected to some sort of severe mental or physical torture as in a hazing situation."[114]

A matter to watch in this regard involves an African American graduate student from the University of Akron. In 2004, the student was arrested on suspicion of drug trafficking, but was acquitted by a jury after presenting an alibi. Later, however, the university's Student Judicial Affairs hearing board found him "responsible for selling drugs to a confidential informant" and suspended him for a semester in September 2004. The school also banned him permanently from the residence halls and indicated that he would have to reapply for the tuition waiver and stipend he originally had been awarded. The ex-student committed suicide in 2005.[115] According to published reports, the family blames the local police and the university for the suicide. At this point, the university is conducting an internal investigation, and the NAACP has called for a grand-jury investigation regarding the police procedures employed. Although the student's father has been quoted that he does not have standing to sue the university,[116] the verdict, so to speak, is still out, as the statute of limitations has not expired.

The other exception to the general rule that third parties are not liable for a person's suicide concerns "duty to prevent" the suicide. Under this exception, courts consider whether a special relationship exists between the defendant and individual who committed suicide. Most frequently, a special relationship involving a highly controlled custodial and controlled situation—such as a jail, hospital, or reform school—makes the defendant more responsible for preventing a suicide.[117] In addition, on occasion, courts equate special knowledge and experience with the type and degree of control sufficient to impose a duty to prevent suicide, which means that mental hospitals, psychiatrists, and other trained mental health professionals might be at risk.[118] However, "'commentators have suggested that imposing liability [on a psychiatrist] . . . is only appropriate if his patient is hospitalized at the time of the suicide, because a psychiatrist does not have *sufficient control* over the non-hospitalized patient to prevent his suicide.'"[119] Under this exception, colleges and universities must be aware of situations that can create a custodial relationship, such as within a campus police station or a university hospital or clinic.[120]

Universities should be aware that the traditional exceptions that have shielded them and their officials from liability for student suicides in a broader range of cases may be eroding.[121] Because schools often settle cases involving student suicides, only a few published cases exist in the area and even fewer reach the merits in terms of liability. Thus, the crystal ball is not clear as to what the future of college and university liability in this area will be, but universities should no longer assume that liability will attach only when one of the two traditional exceptions to the "no proximate causation" rule is established.

Jain v. Iowa (2000) is a student suicide case that was decided on the merits.[122] In *Jain*, a college freshman, Sanjay Jain, began to contemplate suicide after his academic performance declined and he was involved in multiple disciplinary matters. Campus officials became aware of Jain's intentions after finding him and his girlfriend fighting over the keys to his moped. The girlfriend told resident assistants (RAs) that Jain was planning to commit suicide by moving his moped into his residence hall room and inhaling exhaust fumes; Jain confirmed this plan. After Jain assured the RAs he would seek counseling the next day, the RAs left. The next day, Jain met with the hall coordinator, who urged him to seek help at the university counseling center and demanded that Jain remove the moped from his room. University officials also asked Jain for permission to contact his parents. Jain refused, but indicated he would talk to his family during the Thanksgiving break, which was scheduled to start the next day. The hall coordinator reported the incident to appropriate supervisors, but indicated that Jain seemed more tired than hopeless. The university took no further action. While at home for Thanksgiving, Jain did not speak with his parents. When Jain returned to school, he took the moped into his room and told his roommate that he would kill himself when the roommate was not there. When the roommate went away for the weekend, Jain killed himself.[123]

Jain's father, acting as administrator of his estate, sued the university for wrongful death, on grounds that it "negligently failed to exercise reasonable care and caution for [Jain's] safety." He also claimed that, had "the university followed its policy of contacting parents when students engaged in self-destructive behavior, the suicide could have been prevented." The university moved for summary judgment, which was granted and affirmed by the Iowa Supreme Court.[124] Instead of arguing that a special relationship existed based on a custodial relationship, the father, among other things, argued that a special relationship arose when the university learned that Jain had a medical or emotional condition that required medical care. The father also argued that because FERPA permits a college or university to disclose otherwise confidential information in an emergency situation and because the university had a parental-notification policy, it had a duty to inform the parents about their son's behavior.[125] The court rejected these arguments and found that the university did not have a special relationship with the student and thus did not have a duty to prevent the suicide.[126]

In *Schieszler v. Ferrum College* (2002), a second-semester freshman, Michael Frentzel, hanged himself in his residence hall room. During Frentzel's first semester, he was involved in several disciplinary matters and was required to enroll in disciplinary workshops and anger-management courses conducted by the dean of student affairs and a local counseling service. During the spring semester, Frentzel had an argument with his girlfriend, to which the campus police and the RA responded. That same day, he sent a note to his girlfriend indicating that he intended to hang himself with his belt. The girlfriend immediately gave the note to the RA and the campus police, who responded and found Frentzel locked in his room. When Frentzel responded, they saw bruises on his head and neck, which he acknowledged were self-inflicted. The campus police and RA then called the dean of student affairs, who came to the room, met Frentzel, and had Frentzel sign a statement promising that he would not harm himself. An employee from the local counseling service was then called to meet Frentzel.[127] Three days later, the girlfriend received additional communications indicating that Frentzel was suicidal. The girlfriend contacted the dean of student affairs and the outside counselor, who prevented her from returning to Frentzel's room. The counselor and dean delayed in visiting the room, and when they did, Frentzel was dead.[128]

The student's mother, representing Frentzel's estate, sued the college, the dean of student affairs, and the outside counselor for wrongful death. The complaint alleged that "the defendants 'knew or . . . should have known that Frentzel was likely to attempt to hurt himself if not properly supervised, that they were negligent by failing to take adequate precautions to insure that Frentzel did not hurt himself,' and that Frentzel died as a result."[129]

The defendants moved to dismiss the case arguing, among other things, that only the student was responsible for his suicide, an illegal act in Virginia; the defendants did not have a duty to take steps to prevent the student from killing himself; and that the defendants did not cause the student's death.[130] The district court denied the defendants' motion. In the analysis, the court stated that "[w]hile it is unlikely that Virginia would conclude that a special relationship exists as a matter of law between colleges and universities and their students, it might find that a special relationship exists *on the particular facts alleged in this case*."[131] Those facts included the student living in an on-campus residence hall; the defendants' knowledge of the student's emotional problems; the school's requirement that he attend anger-management counseling before permitting him to return for his second semester; school officials' knowledge that soon before his death he had self-inflicted bruises on his head; their knowledge, through the girlfriend, of communications reflecting suicidal ideation; and the requirement imposed by the dean of student affairs that the student sign a statement promising not to harm himself. Based on these alleged facts, the court determined that "the jury could conclude there was 'an imminent probability' that [the student] would try to hurt himself, and that the defendants had notice of this specific harm." Thus, the plaintiff had alleged facts sufficient to support her claim that a special relationship existed between the student and the defendants that gave rise to a duty for the defendants to protect the student from the foreseeable danger that he would hurt himself.[132] The court also found that some of the defendants breached their duty to assist the student, even though they did not have custody and control over him,[133] and indicated that the defendants' failure to ensure that the student was supervised could have been a cause of the suicide.[134] Following this decision, the matter was settled when the college acknowledged it was partly responsible for the student's death.[135]

In 2005, a Massachusetts trial court ruled on a much-anticipated motion for summary judgment in the closely watched case of *Shin v. Massachusetts Institute of Technology* (2005).[136] Elizabeth Shin exhibited serious mental problems over the course of three semesters. During this time, she was evaluated by many trained mental health professionals at MIT facilities and had contact with several non-medical administrators who were aware of her condition, checked on her, and attempted to work with her. She was hospitalized on multiple occasions for suicide attempts and suicidal ideation, and on at least two occasions, her parents were informed of the situation and took her home. Shin admitted that she had mental health issues before entering MIT and acknowledged that she was a cutter. During the three semesters, her mental state fluctuated and was exacerbated by poor academic performance and conflicts with her boyfriend.

After spring break of her sophomore year, matters deteriorated and her need for treatment became more acute. For several weeks, Shin's housemaster received frequent reports from other students that her mental health was deteriorating. Campus officials had frequent contact with her during this period; for example, on one day, she had two treatment sessions with an MIT psychiatrist. On April 8, Shin informed another student that she was going to kill herself with a knife. The student contacted the campus police and officers transported Shin to the health center, where she was evaluated by a staff physician and spoke with the on-call psychiatrist for a few minutes. After the psychiatrist determined that Shin was not suicidal, she was allowed to return to her residence hall room.[137]

At 12:30 a.m. on April 10, students notified the housemaster that Shin had threatened to kill herself that day and had asked one of the students to erase her computer files. The housemaster had contact with Shin that day and believed her threat to be credible. She then relayed this information to the on-call psychiatrist, who said that it was not necessary to bring Shin to the health center because he had spoken with her just two days earlier. The housemaster also contacted the counseling dean, who discussed the matter at the 11:00 a.m. "deans and psychs" meeting, which was attended by several professionals who had treated Shin. After that meeting, a dean left Shin a phone message that she was to report for an appointment the next day. That evening, firefighters extracted a severely burned Shin from her residence hall room. She was taken to the hospital and died a few days later. The medical examiner concluded that the cause of death was "self-inflicted thermal burns."[138]

Shin's parents sued MIT and several MIT administrators, including trained mental health professionals, deans, campus police, and the housemaster, seeking more than $27 million.[139] The defendants moved for summary judgment on various grounds. MIT's motion, which concerned primarily contract-based claims, was granted. The other defendants, however, had mixed luck. First, the court refused to dismiss the claims against the medical professionals for gross negligence. The plaintiffs alleged that the professionals failed to coordinate Shin's care and failed to respond quickly enough in response to her April 10 suicide plan; the court found that these allegations were sufficient to raise a genuine issue of material fact regarding whether the professionals had been grossly negligent in treating Shin.[140] Second, the court refused to dismiss the claims against the non-medical administrators, who argued that they did not owe Shin a duty to prevent her from committing suicide, finding that at least some of the officials who had frequent contact with Shin could have reasonably foreseen that, without proper supervision, Shin would hurt herself. Based on this foreseeability, the court found that a special relationship existed between the administrators and Shin that imposed on them "a duty . . . to exercise reasonable care to protect [Shin] from harm."[141] The court also allowed the gross negligence and wrongful death claims against the administrators to move forward because there was no evidence that the administrators formulated or enacted an immediate plan to deal with Shin's April 10 threats.[142]

Although the opinion gained significant attention because of the "special relationship" analysis, it is important to remember that while the court concluded that many of the individual defendants owed Shin a duty, the court did not rule that any defendant breached that duty, as breach is a fact question for the jury to determine. In April 2006, MIT announced that the case had been settled for a confidential amount.[143]

COLLEGE AND UNIVERSITY RESPONSES TO STUDENT SUICIDE AND THREATS OF SUICIDE

Other cases currently are pending against institutions and institution officials as a result of student suicides,[144] and one case is pending in which a father sued university officials after his daughter died from a heroin overdose.[145] Although it is likely that some or all of these cases will settle before decisions on the merits, it is possible that the higher education community will receive additional guidance on this important, and evolving, area. In the interim, colleges and universities should understand that at least some courts seem to be looking for ways to find a special relationship between students and universities (including individual administrators) and may find that clinical and non-clinical school officials owe a duty to take steps to prevent foreseeable student suicides.

In this climate, universities should carefully review their policies and procedures for responding to students who manifest suicidal ideation or self-destructive behavior. One recent resource that should prove helpful to many universities is the Jed Foundation's 2006 *Framework for Developing Institutional Protocols for the Acutely Distressed or Suicidal Student*, which is available for download on the organization's Web site. The safest approach legally would be to assume that a duty exists to assist a student who has manifested self-destructive behavior, including suicide ideation, and to take reasonable steps to prevent that behavior. These steps might include physically controlling the individual in a way that he or she is not able to complete the suicide—such as admitting the student to a health facility equipped to deal with this type of situation. It might also include notifying parents, other family members, or law enforcement.[146] In some situations, it might involve exploring involuntary hospitalization. In these situations, the institution must balance the students' right to privacy against the risk of harm to the student or others. As outlined in the section on confidentiality, a college student's records generally are protected by federal and state statutes; in addition, the records and condition of a student being treated by licensed physicians and mental health professionals are also protected by rules of confidentiality based on law and ethical standards. That being said, student health and safety trumps privacy in virtually every case.

Campus officials have options that would allow them to abide by the privacy laws and protect student safety. First, as explained in the section on confidentiality, FERPA allows disclosure in a health or safety emergency. Moreover, FERPA covers student records, not observations about student behavior and conduct. In addition, student records can be released if a student consents. In *Shin*, for example, the student permitted campus officials to contact her parents on multiple occasions. Another alternative is to urge the student to contact a family member; if voluntary contact is selected, campus officials should determine a way to verify that the contact has been made—such as asking to stay in the room during the call, or asking to speak briefly with the family member at the end of the call. Sometimes, however, the institution must make a difficult choice. If so, it is important to consider which potential lawsuit the institution would prefer to defend: a lawsuit regarding breach of a student's privacy or a lawsuit concerning failure to protect or failure to prevent a suicide. That answer, hopefully, is self-evident.

Some universities have developed parental notification policies regarding students who use illegal drugs, violate alcohol laws or policies, or engage in self-destructive behavior.[147] This disclosure is permitted under the Higher Education Act of 1999, and, for students under 18, by FERPA. Although the Iowa Supreme Court in *Jain* did not hold the university liable for failing to report the student's suicide ideation under the parental notification policy, some courts may be willing to find that, under a particular set of circumstances, such policies add to the institution's duty to assist the student.

This development does not mean that universities should shy away from notification policies. Instead, it means that universities should carefully examine, and possibly re-craft, their policies to give campus administrators the ability to exercise appropriate discretion and to comfortably use the policy when, in light of their expertise and training, they believe they can help a student. For example, contacting a particular family member might actually exacerbate the student's condition, if that person is a cause of the student's troubles. A parent might, for instance, be physically, verbally, or emotionally abusive, and that parent's treatment of the student might be a root cause of the student's depression or suicidal thoughts. Trained administrators must have the ability *not* to notify that parent in that situation. In another situation, the administrator might learn that the parents are well aware of the student's condition, having dealt with it for many years, and, now that the student is in college, have no intention of intervening. In this situation, the administrator may determine that parental notification will have no positive consequence and should discuss other options with the student, such as checking into a mental health facility. On the other hand, an administrator who truly believes that a family member should be notified of the student's situation and has no reason to believe it would be harmful, should not fear to make that call—hopefully after speaking with the student, if circumstances permit. Senior leaders on campus should set the tone that health and safety come before other concerns.

Shin also teaches us that campus officials must coordinate their efforts concerning troubled students, and might be required to act expeditiously under certain circumstances. In response to the *Shin* suit and other recent student suicides, MIT enhanced its mental health policies and, among other things, extended the hours for mental health services, "hired additional mental health staff fluent in languages other than English[,] and enhanced coordination of mental health and medical care with other departments on campus, from athletics to the chaplain's office, and from the disabilities office to residential life."[148] Schools that do not have on-campus mental health resources might consider entering into memoranda of understanding or other arrangements with external organizations or individuals, such as local hospitals or mental health professionals, who may be able to assess or care for a student at risk for suicide.[149]

A related issue concerns how campus officials document encounters with acutely distressed students. In this regard, the institution should seek input from legal counsel regarding when and how to record such communications and contact, and how such reports can and should be shared, used, and stored.[150]

In light of the "duty" language in *Shin*, some administrators might sense that they should try to avoid creating a special relationship by shying away from students and their problems. That, however, is not the message. Administrators cannot be ostriches who bury their heads in the sand, especially when it comes to student health and safety. Foreseeability, which is a key for some courts in determining that a special relationship exists, is based on a "knew or should have known" standard. Accordingly, purposely insulating oneself from knowledge will not absolve a campus administrator from liability.

The Facilitator Model and its emphasis on shared responsibility proves helpful in this context. "A facilitator university does not view the student's wellness as a student-health-services issue only."[151] Instead, a Facilitator University recognizes that college is a period of transition for students who are not yet fully developed adults. As such, they "need structure and an environment in which they can make reasonable, safe choices."[152] On an operational level, this means that the institution will provide an array of services, including health care, spiritual programs, and wellness programs, and will "foster an environment in which a student at risk of suicide will be protected by the entire community, including fellow students."[153] This may include involving friends and family when the student is in crisis, offering awareness programs on campus and for families, and training staff about how to identify and work with students who are depressed and showing signs of suicide ideation. It also means discussing with students whether it is better for them to leave the community for a period to receive help or to remain on campus while receiving help. This discussion can often be difficult, as the students at issue are often high achievers who may view leaving college as a failure. The institution also should have access to professionals who can work with students to help them see the long-term benefits of a short-term leave of absence.

Another issue that has gained recent attention is whether a college or university can or should dismiss a student who exhibits severe depression or suicide ideation. A situation that has garnered recent press concerns a former George Washington University student who has sued the university and several administrators.[154] The student, who lost a close friend and fellow GW student to suicide, started to feel depressed and to think about suicide. He sought counseling and later checked himself into the university hospital. Within hours of checking into the hospital, he received a letter from the university barring him from the residence halls; a day later, he received another letter indicating that his "endangering behavior" violated the code of student conduct. The letter stated that he faced suspension and expulsion from school, unless he withdrew while in treatment. The letter also notified him that he was barred from campus.[155] The student opted not to proceed with a conduct hearing, but instead withdrew, enrolled in another college, and filed suit.

The lawsuit names the university and many administrators, including the president, the executive vice president for academic affairs, the dean of students, the assistant dean of students, the director of the counseling center, the director and assistant director of student judicial services, the chief of police, the chief executive officer of the hospital, and some individual doctors.[156] The causes of action are based on the Americans with Disabilities Act, Section 504 of the Rehabilitation Act, the Fair Housing Amendments Act of 1988, and the District of Columbia's human rights act.[157] The defendants have denied liability and specifically have stated that the counseling center and medical personnel did not share the student's information with university administrators. Instead, GW contends that a friend, relative, or someone else notified administrators about the student's condition.[158] Although the higher education community should watch this case carefully, the Office of Civil Rights has issued rulings in similar situations.

For example, in 2005, the OCR determined that Marietta College had violated Section 504 of the Rehabilitation Act for dismissing a student after he and his parents shared information about his depression and history of suicide attempts with a staff psychologist, who in turn reported the information to the dean.[159] The school indicated that it felt the student posed a direct threat to health and safety on campus and dismissed him pursuant to its emergency withdrawal policy. The assessment of direct threat was based on the student's unwillingness to participate in weekly counseling, the fact that past suicide attempts occurred without warning, and a report from the student's roommate that he was acting strangely and talking frequently about death. The day that the psychologist spoke with the dean, he saw the student, who indicated that monthly counseling was sufficient and that he was feeling fine. During a meeting a couple of days later, the student boasted to the psychologist that if he were going to commit suicide, no one would ever know. The psychologist believed this statement constituted a threat that the student was going to kill himself. In a subsequent meeting with the student's parents, college officials suggested that the student withdraw voluntarily. When the student and parents rejected that offer, the college invoked its emergency withdrawal policy, which indicated that students who threaten or attempt suicide may be involuntarily withdrawn from the college.[160]

In finding the violation, the OCR explained that:

> [a]lthough Section 504 does not prohibit a postsecondary education institution from taking action to address an imminent risk of danger posed by an individual with a disability who represents a direct threat to the health and safety of himself/herself or others, *such action must be grounded in sound evidence and cannot be based on unfounded fears, prejudice, or stereotypes regarding individuals with psychiatric disabilities* to ensure that such individuals are not discriminated against because of their disability. *To rise to the level of a direct threat, there must be a high probability of substantial harm and not just a slightly increased, speculative, or remote risk.* In a direct threat situation, a postsecondary education institution *needs to make an individualized and objective assessment of the student's ability to safely participate in the institution's program based on a reasonable medical judgment relying on the most current medical knowledge*

or *the best available objective evidence*. The assessment must determine the nature, duration, and severity of the risk; the probability that the potentially threatening injury will actually occur; and whether reasonable modifications of policies, practices, or procedures will sufficiently mitigate the risk. Due process requires a postsecondary institution to adhere to procedures that ensure that students with disabilities are not subject to adverse action on the basis of unfounded fear, prejudice, or stereotypes. *A nondiscriminatory belief must be based on observation of a student's conduct, actions, and statements, not merely knowledge or beliefs that a student is an individual with a disability.* In exceptional circumstances, such as situations where safety is of immediate concern, a college may take interim steps pending a final decision regarding an adverse action against a student as long as minimal due process, such as notice and an opportunity to address the evidence, is provided in the interim and full due process, including a hearing and the right to appeal, is offered later.[161]

Using this standard, the OCR determined that the information the college possessed at the time of the involuntary withdrawal "was not sufficient to demonstrate the existence of the type of high probability of substantial harm to the Student, as opposed to a slightly increased or speculative risk, necessary to support a direct threat defense."[162] Specifically, OCR criticized the college for not conducting an individualized, objective assessment of the student's ability to participate safely in the college's program, "based on a reasonable medical judgment, and did not consider whether the perceived risk of injury to the Student could have been mitigated by reasonable modifications of College policies, practices, or procedures."[163] The OCR also found "that the College [did] not have a grievance procedure for disability discrimination complaints, or a Section 504 coordinator, as required by" regulation.[164]

The college agreed to voluntarily resolve the complaint by designating a trained Section 504 coordinator and publicizing the coordinator's services, offering the student readmission, amending its emergency withdrawal policy to, among other things, indicate that a decision "to subject a student with a disability to an emergency withdrawal will be made in consultation with persons knowledgeable about the College's obligations under Federal disability civil rights laws and direct threat standards," and to develop a disability discrimination grievance procedure.

This and similar rulings[165] could discourage and frustrate some campus administrators, as it seems to second-guess their best efforts to promote health and safety on campus. Some lessons that schools should draw from the OCR rulings include that trained medical and mental health professionals should be involved in the decision-making process whenever possible; evaluation of the student's mental condition must be individualized and must not be cursory; and dismissing the student involuntarily, and especially without a policy that defines "direct threat" or a mechanism to appeal that decision, rarely should be the institution's first step in working with a troubled student. It is important to remember, however, that trained administrators must use their best judgment in issues of campus health and safety, and that courts are less likely than the OCR to second-guess their decisions when made in a reasonable manner. It is also important to remember that, absent a pattern of conduct, an OCR inquiry often can be resolved voluntarily and informally, and without the expenditure of significant campus resources. Accordingly, when balancing interests and options, student health and safety remain paramount.

From a policy perspective, universities might consider the program of mandated assessment implemented by the University of Illinois in 1984. This program, which requires any student who threatens or attempts suicide to attend four counseling sessions, has resulted in a 58% reduction in suicide rates at the University. The program, run by Paul Joffe, treats suicide as an act of violence, not an act of helplessness. More than 2,000 students have participated in the program, and not one has committed suicide. The program has the benefits of professional input and individual evaluation. In addition, consistent with the Facilitator Model, the program requires the student to share responsibility for his circumstances and future, because a student is not dismissed unless he refuses to participate in the program.[166]

STUDENTS WHO POSE A DANGER TO OTHERS

The Legal Environment

Students may pose a danger to others in many ways: Some threaten to injure others, some intentionally injure others without warning, and others bully or stalk.[167] Civil cases in which the institution or its employees are sued for injury or death involving a student's conduct typically found in negligence: negligent admission, negligent failure to provide adequate security, negligent failure to warn, and so forth. In these cases, the plaintiff bears the burden of proving that the institution or its officials owed the plaintiff a duty, that they breached that duty, that injury was caused by the act or omission of the institution or its employees, and that the plaintiff suffered damages as a result. In most contexts, courts hold that the institution and its officials must use reasonable care to protect students from foreseeable danger. What constitutes reasonable care and foreseeable danger are fact-intensive questions; thus, the outcomes in cases differ, with some resulting in liability and others resulting in no liability.

The seminal university case involving a student with a mental illness who posed a threat to another is *Tarasoff v. Regents of the University of California* (1976).[168] In *Tarasoff*, a graduate student confided in the university psychologist that he intended to kill an unnamed, but identifiable, woman, who was the sister of his roommate, when she returned home after the summer. The doctor decided that the student should be committed to a mental hospital for observation and asked campus police to take the student into custody, which they did. However, the officers released him after determining that he was rational and he promised to stay away from the woman. The doctor took no further action to place the student into treatment and did not warn the woman or her parents that she was in danger.[169] Thereafter, the student killed the woman. Her parents, as representatives of her estate, sued the university and several individuals, including university psychologists.

The California Supreme Court held that "once a therapist does in fact determine, or under applicable professional standards reasonably should have determined, that a patient poses a serious danger of violence to others, he bears a duty to exercise reasonable care to protect the foreseeable victim of that danger."[170] The Court also explained that "this duty . . . will necessarily vary with the facts of each case,"[171] and may require the therapist "to warn the intended victim or others likely to apprise the victim of the danger, to notify the police, or to take whatever other steps are reasonably necessary under the circumstances."[172]

Most jurisdictions have treated *Tarasoff* favorably. Only a few courts have rejected *Tarasoff*, and in at least two of those instances, the state legislature abrogated the case with a statute imposing a duty to warn.[173]

Another landmark case concerning an institution's duty to protect students from dangerous persons is *Mullins v. Pine Manor College* (1983).[174] In *Mullins*, a female student was raped in her residence hall room by an unidentified assailant. Abrogating traditional common law, the Massachusetts Supreme Judicial Court held that the college had a duty to exercise reasonable care to protect students from criminal acts of third parties.[175] The court based this conclusion on a variety of grounds, including determinations that criminal behavior on campus was foreseeable and that the college controlled key aspects of campus safety, such as installing a security system, hiring security guards, setting a patrol policy, installing locks, etc.[176]

In *Nero v. Kansas State University* (1993),[177] the rule in *Mullins* was extended to require a university to protect students against the dangerous acts of other students. In *Nero*, a male student was accused of raping a female student in a co-ed residence hall on campus in which they both lived. Following the rape accusation and pending resolution of the criminal case, the male student was reassigned to live in an all-male residence hall on the other side of campus; the student also was directed not to enter any co-ed or all-female residence halls. The student registered for spring intersession and was assigned to a co-ed residence hall, which was the only residence hall open. A few weeks later, he sexually assaulted Shana Nero, a female resident of that hall.

Nero sued the university for negligence for failing to protect her from the sexual assault or warning her about the male student and his past conduct.[178] The court held that while "a university is not an insurer of the safety of its students," it "has a duty [to use] reasonable care to protect its students against certain dangers, including criminal actions against a student by another student or a third party if the criminal act is reasonably foreseeable and within the university's control."[179] Because the university was aware of the prior rape charge, moved him to an all-male residence hall, and prohibited him from entering co-ed and all-female residence halls, the court determined that the attack was foreseeable and that the university had not exercised reasonable care under the circumstances.[180]

Although a college or university may have a duty to use reasonable care to protect a student from foreseeable harm, the student must also take reasonable steps to protect himself. For example, in *Rhaney v. University of Maryland Eastern Shore* (2005),[181] the court held that the university was not liable in negligence for student-on-student violence. There, Clark punched his roommate, breaking his jaw. Clark had been suspended from the school earlier for fighting at an on-campus party. The injured roommate sued the university for, among other things, negligently failing to warn him about Clark's dangerous tendencies and negligently assigning Clark to be his roommate. The court identified various reasons why the university was not liable, the last of which was lack of foreseeability. The lack of foreseeability was based in part on the fact that the injured roommate was aware of Clark's past violence on campus, lived with him for two months, and did not request a new roommate. As part of this analysis, the court referred to the injured roommate's failure to "exercise ordinary care for this own safety."[182]

Similarly, in *Lloyd v. Alpha Phi Alpha Fraternity* (1999),[183] a student's negligence action against Cornell University for injuries suffered during fraternity hazing was dismissed on various grounds, including that the student not only failed to alert the university about the alleged abuse, but concealed the activity by lying to campus officials about the true source of his injuries. The court stated that if the university was unable to learn about the hazing through the individual student or others, "then it is contrary to common sense to think a duty could be imposed upon the University to protect persons against these unknown activities."[184]

Another trend that may be emerging involves lawsuits for the negligent admission of dangerous students. Two suits recently were filed by the father of student Jessica Faulkner, who was murdered at the University of North Carolina-Wilmington. One complaint names as the defendant the father of the student who committed the murder; the father is also an administrator in the University of North Carolina system. His son had been expelled from another UNC campus following a stalking incident in which he brandished a knife in a female student's residence hall room. The father allegedly completed the son's application and did not reveal this or other information about his son's past troubles. At the time of the incident, UNC did not have a procedure to conduct background checks on applicants for admission.[185] The second suit, against the university, is pending before the North Carolina Industrial Commission, as the law requires.[186]

Following the murder of Jessica Faulkner and the unrelated murder of another student, the university created a system-wide safety task force that urged more careful screening of admissions applicants. Although the university does not yet conduct checks on all applicants, it has developed a list of "red flags" on an application that will trigger in a full background check. These include an unexplained gap between high-school graduation and the application for admission, significant grade fluctuations, or withdrawals.[187] In addition, the state legislature is currently considering a bill that will require background checks for every admitted student.[188] In a similar vein, the Virginia legislature recently enacted legislation that will require colleges and universities in the state to submit personal information about all accepted applicants to the state police to be checked against registries of sex offenders.[189]

COLLEGE AND UNIVERSITY ACTIONS AND RESPONSES

What can be gleaned from recent cases is that universities are subject to normal tort liabilities and in most cases are not treated deferentially, but are, more than ever before, treated like other businesses.[190] Accordingly, institutions and their officials owe students a reasonable duty of care to protect them from foreseeable harm, including the criminal acts of dangerous students and other third parties. Also, under *Tarasoff* and its progeny, licensed mental health officials in most jurisdictions have duties to warn and/or to protect identifiable victims of harm.

The questions, therefore, become "what is foreseeable" and "what does 'reasonable care' mean?" One way for universities to begin to address these questions is to establish a collaborative risk-management team on campus that (a) identifies risks of all sorts, ranging from risks in the admissions process to risks in residence life and student activities to risks associated with facilities and the physical campus; (b) generates solutions to prevent or minimize the risks; (c) selects the best solution or solution set for each risk; (d) implements the solution, which often includes education and training; and (e) on a regular basis, evaluates and adjusts the solutions.[191] Engaging in this process will help universities identify what types of risks are foreseeable and will help identify reasonable solutions to protect the health, safety, and welfare of the campus community.

In addition, campus administrators must not be islands unto themselves. Instead, the college or university must develop ways to share information across departments. For example, it is common that a student who has been referred to the office of student life or to the judicial council for non-academic misconduct is experiencing academic difficulties as well. On some campuses, however, representatives from academic affairs, student life, and the judicial council do not formally or informally meet or otherwise share information. If they did, the chances of stopping dangerous and other problematic behavior would increase. Therefore, it is crucial that universities create ways for administrators and faculty to share information and develop joint solutions for working with students. These teams also must be flexible enough to respond to situations that demand quick action, such as students who have threatened suicide or who have manifested otherwise dangerous conduct. In these situations, campus officials must act quickly, must not wait for regularly scheduled meetings to share information and make decisions, and must remember that health and safety are paramount concerns when balancing myriad factors that arise during crises or potential crises.

Discipline

As in other contexts involving students with mental impairments, universities must abide by Section 504 of the Rehabilitation Act and the Americans with Disabilities Act. However, universities need not tolerate behavior that runs counter to their discipline codes or policies regarding health and safety. When the behavior of a student with a mental disability has no connection to that disability, the college or university can and should treat that student as it would nondisabled students. For example, if the student engages in illegal drug use or fails to reveal a prior criminal record,[192] the college or university typically should follow its regular policies and procedures when dealing with that student.

In addition, a college or university may discipline a student for violating a code provision designed to maintain a safe and orderly campus, even if the student's misconduct results from a disability. For example, a law school expelled a student with bipolar disorder who threatened "to blow up the legal writing department" and physically intimidated a professor. The student argued that the conduct resulted from his disability. The OCR concluded that the school treated the student as it would any other student who behaved in a similar manner and did not discriminate against the student based on his disability.[193]

A similar standard can be applied to academic misconduct. A nursing student with ADHD was provided with extended time and a quiet place to take his examination. During one exam, campus officials observed the student engaging in misconduct, including using an unauthorized calculator, using a cell phone, and going to the restroom 13 times. The student's grade was lowered after disabilities services staff determined that the student had cheated on the examination. The OCR determined that the discipline was imposed based on the student's misconduct and that the allegations of misconduct were not based on the student's disability or request for accommodations.[194]

Courts also afford great deference to universities to dismiss students on academic grounds. In most cases, the court defers to the professional judgment of the faculty in determining whether the student has met the fundamental requirements of the program.[195] In addition, when a college or university dismisses a student who has not disclosed the disability, courts are loathe to hold the institution liable under the disability laws.[196]

Despite what the law permits, universities should strive to use disciplinary processes as educational tools to assist students in their personal and professional development. Officials who administer the discipline system should work with students holistically and should seek interdisciplinary solutions to students' problems. They should act primarily as educators and mentors, as opposed to prosecutors and jurists. Just as forcing suicidal students to withdraw is not necessarily the most effective first step in that situation, imposing sanctions on a disabled student without understanding his or her disability and its manifestations—and without attempting to teach the student why the conduct at issue was not acceptable or responsible—is contrary to most universities' educational missions.

When students do request appropriate accommodations in the context of a dismissal, universities, at a minimum, should evaluate those requests carefully.[197] In two recent cases, a federal court ruled that a medical school violated the ADA. In one case, the institution denied the student's request to postpone a decision on his academic dismissal so that a recently diagnosed learning disability could be considered. In the second case, the institution denied the student's request for reconsideration of a committee's dismissal recommendation after she discovered and documented that she had a learning disability.[198]

Universities can run afoul of the law if they discipline a student with a disability more harshly than they have disciplined non-disabled students for the same conduct. In addition, a school may not discipline a student in retaliation for engaging in protected activity, such as requesting an accommodation under Section 504 or the ADA or filing a grievance for disability discrimination. Finally, as in other situations involving discipline, universities should strive to follow the procedures set forth in their policies and codes; most critically, they should provide the student with notice and an opportunity to be heard.

When a student with a disability participates in a disciplinary or judicial process on campus, the student may be entitled to reasonable accommodations related to his or her disability. For example, in one case, a community college denied a student's request for additional time to prepare for a hearing but granted her request to delay the hearing so that her parents could attend and help to facilitate communication. The OCR found that the college did not have to grant the requested accommodation of additional time because it did not relate to the student's disability and commended the college on granting the request for the parent to attend.[199] In addition, experts advise that students with disabilities should be reminded about the school's honor and conduct codes and their obligation to abide by those codes.[200]

With regard to students who pose a danger to others, in addition to considering an involuntary leave policy, universities might also consider adding the ability to suspend students on an interim basis while an investigation or evaluation is pending, or the ability to remove students from campus housing.[201]

Universities also should consider the value of adding educational conferences to their disciplinary codes. An educational conference provides campus officials with the ability to address a student's behavior that is inappropriate or disruptive, but that does not yet rise to the level of a disciplinary violation. This type of conference, which is consistent with most universities' educational missions, allows campus officials to work with students who have special abilities and challenges, and also to have the student enter into a conduct agreement, the violation of which may carry sanctions. Educational conferences are consistent with the concepts of instruction and shared responsibility under the Facilitator Model.

To reiterate, when dealing with students with disabilities, the focus should be on the behavior, and not the disability, and the focus on behavior must not be pretextual, which means that the focus on behavior as opposed to disability must be genuine.[202] Further, education, values, and principles—not sanctions and punishment—should be the primary goals of the discipline system.

Readmission

As with admissions decisions, universities must be cognizant of Section 504 and the ADA when deciding whether a student with a mental disability should be readmitted. A frequently cited readmissions case involving a student with a mental disability is *Doe v. New York University* (1981).[203] In this case, Doe was admitted to the School of Medicine at New York University (NYU) after falsely representing on her admissions application that she did not suffer from any chronic or recurrent illnesses or emotional problems. She actually suffered from "serious psychiatric and mental disorders, which evidenced themselves in the form of numerous self-destructive acts and attacks upon others."[204] All students admitted to the School of Medicine were required to undergo a medical examination during their first month. When the doctor examined Doe, who had delayed the examination for many weeks, he noticed scars and asked about their cause; for the first time, she revealed some of her psychiatric history. The doctor recommended that Doe undergo a psychiatric examination. After initially refusing, she met with a university psychiatrist, provided a more detailed history, and underwent additional tests. Despite conclusions that Doe suffered from a mental disorder, the School of Medicine agreed to allow her stay on the condition that she agreed to psychiatric treatment, which she did. Doe, however, once again engaged in self-destructive behavior and was granted a leave of absence with the understanding that she might seek reinstatement, but that reinstatement was not guaranteed.[205]

About 18 months later, Doe applied for readmission; her application was supported by two psychiatrists who had treated her in the interim. After reviewing her complete treatment file for the interim period, NYU denied her application. Later that year, under threat of legal action, NYU agreed to reconsider its decision and to interview Doe. The interviewer, an associate professor of clinical psychiatry, concluded that Doe suffered from the same conditions that she did at the time her leave was granted and recommended against readmission on grounds that she posed an unreasonable risk to faculty, students, and patients. Doe then sued NYU for alleged violation of Section 504 of the Rehabilitation Act and asked to be reinstated.[206] Although the trial court ordered NYU to reinstate her, the appellate court reversed and found for NYU. The appellate court found that although Doe was not readmitted because of her disability, Doe was not an "otherwise qualified applicant" because of the serious nature of her disorder and the danger she posed to herself and others. The court also held that the medical school, in determining whether she was qualified, could consider her mental disorder, along with all other relevant factors. Moreover, the court emphasized that the academic judgment of the medical school was to be afforded great deference.[207]

Subsequent cases have reiterated that, on readmission, the institution can consider the applicant's mental disorder along with other relevant factors. For example, in *Hash v. University of Kentucky* (2004),[208] the university properly considered the student's past history of depression, the fact that his application for readmission was untimely, the applicant's personal statement and other writings that raised questions about his mental stability, and correspondence from professors and doctors. The OCR has also found in favor of universities when applicants for readmission have not met the school's non-discriminatory standard for readmission.[209] The OCR has also determined that a college or university can require a student with a mental disability to submit a psychiatric evaluation as part of the readmissions process, if the institution has legitimate concerns for campus health and safety based on the student's past conduct.[210]

Also in the area of readmissions, a college or university should not be held liable under the disability laws if those who deny the application have no knowledge of the student's disability.[211] In addition, a college or university has no obligation to readmit a dismissed student who later learns he has a disability.[212]

In sum, colleges and universities legally may deny applications for readmission from disabled students when (a) the institution is not aware of the disability, (b) readmission is denied on the same ground that would have been used for a similarly situated non-disabled student, or (c) the former student is not an "otherwise qualified person," taking into consideration the disability and all other relevant factors. Courts and the OCR are particularly deferential to an institution's decision not to readmit when the safety of the applicant, other students, faculty, and members of the campus community are legitimately at risk, as supported by professional assessments in the file, and when the faculty exercises non-discriminatory academic judgment.

Incorporating the Facilitator Model, the college or university would hold the student seeking readmission responsible for fulfilling any prerequisites to readmission. It also would seek information to help campus officials to determine, to the best of their abilities, whether the student presents a danger to himself or herself, or to others. For students who still present a direct threat, the Facilitator University would opt not to readmit that student, even if the student threatened legal action. In close cases, the Facilitator University would explore creative alternatives.[213] For example, it might readmit the student on a probationary basis, with conditions, while it continued to evaluate and monitor the situation. The student might be permitted to attend a limited number of on-campus courses, take some courses by distance learning, be prohibited from living in the residence halls, or be required to meet regularly with a disability-service coordinator, mental health counselor, or academic-support professional, who would in turn coordinate closely with the dean of students and the dean of academics. The Facilitator University would, in short, recognize that it should rely on the discretion and expertise of trained professionals who are striving to fulfill the institution's educational mission to create a safe campus environment.

CONCLUSION

Because an escalating number of students with mental disorders and challenges are entering college, faculty and administrators must increase their understanding of at least the most common and the most serious of these conditions. They must also understand the student's and the institution's legal rights and responsibilities. As part of this educational process, it is imperative that institution counsel and trained medical and mental health professionals be integral parts of the dialogue.

It is also essential that universities develop thoughtful methods to work with students who have mental health issues and protocols to respond to emergencies and crises that might result when students pose a danger to themselves or to others. These protocols must be legally and scientifically sound and must be flexible enough to deal with situations that require immediate attention and action. For example, even if campus officials meet weekly to discuss students whose situations they are monitoring, they must be prepared to act more quickly if the circumstances require.

As noted in the introduction, universities should consider adopting the Facilitator Model or another philosophy of the institution's relationship to its students. This type of philosophy can guide the university when establishing policies and procedures and can help determine its response to legal issues. In addition, the model can create a campus culture of shared responsibility, which in turn can help promote improved health and safety on campus.

Finally, institutions should not think simply in terms of avoiding or minimizing the institution's legal liability. The institution's mission is to educate students, and, for many institutions, to help students complete their developmental process and transition into the adult world. Therefore, when addressing issues related to students with mental health challenges, the college or university should first and foremost consider that student's well-being and the safety and well-being of others on campus. If the college or university uses these human-based ideals as its touchstone, its legal position will often be stronger than if it implements policies and procedures merely to avoid liability.

Footnotes

1. Robert P. Gallagher, Monograph Series No. 80, 2005 National Survey of Counseling Center Directors 4 (2005), *available at* http://www.iacsinc.org/2005%20National%20Survey.pdf.

2. Robert D. Bickel & Peter F. Lake, The Rights and Responsibilities of the Modern University: Who Assumes the Risks of College Life? ch. VI (1999).

3. *Id.* at 193 (emphasis in original).

4. 29 U.S.C. § 794 (2000).

5. 42 U.S.C. §§ 12101–12117 (2000).

6. 29 U.S.C. § 794(a); 34 C.F.R. § 104.41 (2006).

7. 34 C.F.R. § 104.3(j)(1).

8. 34 C.F.R. § 104.3(j)(2)(ii).

9. 34 C.F.R. § 104.3(l)(3).

10. 34 C.F.R. § 104.42(b)(2)–(3).

11. St. Thomas Univ. (Fla.), 18 Nat'l Disab. L. Rep. (LRP) ¶ 245 (Office of Civil Rights Region IV Oct. 14, 1999).

12. Univ. of Memphis (Tenn.), 14 Nat'l Disab. L. Rep. (LRP) ¶ 34 (Office of Civil Rights Region IV May 12, 1998).

13. Letter to Northwestern State Univ., No. 06-02-2004 (Office of Civil Rights Chicago Apr. 12, 2002).

14. Univ. of Cincinnati, Complaint No. 15-00-2042, 2000 NDLR (LRP) LEXIS 315; 20 NDLR (LRP) 160 (Office of Civil Rights Oct. 27, 2000) (music conservatory applicant with a learning disability did not meet minimum eligibility requirements because his high school had

waived his foreign-language requirement); Letter to Univ. of Mass. Dartmouth, No. 01-00-2074 (Office of Civil Rights Boston Oct. 16, 2000) (applicant with depression and learning disabilities did not have the required number of college preparatory courses and his GPA was below the required minimum).

15   34 C.F.R. §§ 104.6(b), 104.42(b)(4), 104.42(c).

16   *E.g.* Letter to Oral Roberts Univ., No. 06-01-2037 (Office of Civil Rights Apr. 22, 2002). *But see* Glendale Cmty. College (Ariz.), 1993 NDLR (LRP) LEXIS 1330, 5 NDLR (LRP) 36 (Office of Civil Rights Dec. 16, 1993) (finding that the school's pre-admission disability inquiry violated the regulations, even though the form contained all of the required promises and disclaimers; the form included a list of disabilities with code numbers, and applicants were requested to enter the appropriate codes).

17   34 C.F.R. § 104.42(c).

18   Letter to Cmty. College of S. Nev., Cheyenne Campus, Complaint No. 10-02-2045, 2002 NDLR (LRP) LEXIS 938; 103 LRP 81; 26 NDLR 290 (Office of Civil Rights Western Div. Oct. 18, 2002) (discussed in WHAT DISABILITY SERVICE PROVIDERS SHOULD KNOW ABOUT PSYCHIATRIC DISABILITIES 1–2 (Ed Filo ed., 2003) [hereinafter Psychiatric Disabilities]).

19   Penn. State Univ., Complaint No. 03-91-2020, 1991 NDLR (LRP) LEXIS 1037; 2 NDLR (LRP) 35 (Office of Civil Rights Region III May 3, 1991) (discussed in Adam A. Milani, *Disabled Students in Higher Education*, 22 J.C. & U.L. 989, 999 (1996)).

20   Letter to Univ. of N.C. at Greensboro, No. 04-94-2143 (Office of Civil Rights Region IV 1995).

21   Conception Seminary College (Mo.), 18 Nat'l Disab. L. Rep. (LRP) ¶ 216 (Office of Civil Rights Region VII (2000) (seminary college); N.D. State Univ., Complaint No. 08-91-2001, 1991 NDLR (LRP) LEXIS 1176, 2 NDLR (LRP) 174 (Office of Civil Rights Region VIII Sept. 6, 1991) (counseling program).

22 *E.g.*, Letter to W. Ga. College, No. 04-94-2192 (Office of Civil Rights Region IV 1995) (finding that a nursing program unlawfully required completion of a pre-admission health form).

23 Baird ex rel. Baird v. Rose, 192 F.3d 462, 468–469 (4th Cir. 1999).

24 42 U.S.C. §§ 12161, 12181(7)(J) (2000).

25 28 C.F.R. pts. 35, 36 (2006).

26 28 C.F.R. §§ 35.103(b), 36.103(b).

27 42 U.S.C. § 12131(2); Gent v. Radford Univ., 976 F. Supp. 391, 392 (W.D. Va. 1997), *aff'd*, 122 F.3d 1061 (4th Cir. 1997) (table case).

28 42 U.S.C. § 12102(2)(A).

29 28 C.F.R. §§ 35.104, 36.104.

30 *E.g.*, Webb v. Mercy Hospital, 102 F.3d 958, 960 (8th Cir. 1996); Stewart v. County of Brown, 86 F.3d 107, 111–12 (7th Cir. 1996); Daley v. Koch, 892 F.2d 212, 215 (2d Cir. 1989).

31 42 U.S.C. § 12114, 28 C.F.R. §§ 35.104, 36.104.

32 28 C.F.R. §§ 35.130(8), 36.301.

33 William A. Kaplin & Barbara A. Lee, The Law of Higher Education: A Comprehensive Guide to Legal Implications of Administrative Decision Making § 4.2.4.3 (3d ed. 1995).

34 *See* Cara Cahalan-Laitusis, Ellen B. Mandinach & Wayne J. Camara, *The Impact of Flagging on the Admissions Process*, 181 J. College Admissions, Fall 2003, at 18.

35 These recommendations are based in part on materials located at The Catholic University of America, The Office of General Counsel, *ADA Guidelines: Answer Guide to Self-Audit Checklist*, http://counsel.cua.edu/ada/resources/answers/pre.cfm (last visited Apr. 29, 2006), and

University of Washington, *The Student Services Conference Room, Recruiting and Admissions*, http://www.washington.edu/doit/Conf/recruiting_admissions.html (last visited Apr. 29, 2006).

36   See the discussion above regarding negligent admissions.

37   *See generally* Suzanne Wilhelm, *Accommodating Mental Disabilities in Higher Education: A Practical Guide to ADA Requirements*, 32 J.L. & Educ. 217 (2003).

38   The Catholic Univ. of Am., The Office of Gen. Counsel, *ADA Guidelines: Reasonable Accommodation/Student*, http://counsel.cua.edu/ADA/clicks/reasstu.cfm#Undue (last visited Apr. 29, 2006).

39   Alexander v. Choate, 469 U.S. 287, 302–04 (1985); Southeastern Cmty. College v. Davis, 442 U.S. 397, 409–11 (1979).

40   42 U.S.C. § 12111(10); *see also* 28 C.F.R. §§ 35.164, 36.104; C.F.R. § 104.12(c).

41   42 U.S.C. § 12111(10)(B); The Catholic Univ. of Am., *supra* note 38.

42   42 U.S.C. §§ 12111(3), 12113(d)(3); *see also* Chevron U.S.A. Inc. v. Echazabal, 536 U.S. 73 (2002).

43   173 F.3d 843 (2d Cir. 1999) (table case).

44   *E.g.*, Shaboon v. Duncan, 252 F.3d 722 (5th Cir. 2001); Maczaczyj v. New York, 956 F. Supp. 403 (W.D.N.Y. 1997).

45   Carten v. Kent State Univ., 78 Fed. Appx. 499, 500–01 (6th Cir. 2003) (unpublished); Abdo v. Univ. of Vt., 263 F. Supp. 2d 772, 777–78 (D. Vt. 2003); Wong v. Regents of Univ. of Cal., 192 F.3d 807, 816–17 (9th Cir. 1999) (holding that the student has the initial burden to identify accommodation s; the burden then shifts to the university to demonstrate that the requested accommodations are not reasonable or that the student is not otherwise qualified).

46   *E.g.*, Letter to Tex. Woman's Univ., No. 06-00-2038 (Office of Civil Rights Region VI 2000); Letter to W. Mich. Univ., No. 15-99-2016

(Office of Civil Rights Region XV 2000); Letter to Montgomery College (Md.), No. 03-99-2059 (Office of Civil Rights Region I 1999); *see also* Kaltenberger v. Ohio College of Podiatric Med., 162 F.3d 432, 437 (6th Cir. 1998) (finding that the student's mere statement to an academic advisor that she believed she might have ADHD did not trigger an ADA obligation for the college).

47 Stern v. Univ. of Osteopathic Med. & Health Scis., 220 F.3d 906, 908 (8th Cir. 2000).

48 Letter to Montgomery College (Md.), No. 03-99-2059 (Office of Civil Rights Region I 1999).

49 Regents of Univ. of Mich. v. Ewing, 474 U.S. 214, 225 (1985); Doherty v. Southern College of Optometry, 862 F.2d 570, 575 (6th Cir. 1988) (discussing Section 504); McGuinness v. Univ. of N. Mex. Sch. of Med., 170 F.3d 974, 979 (10th Cir. 1998) (discussing the ADA).

50 *Wong*, 192 F.3d at 818.

51 Psychiatric Disabilities, *supra* note 18, at 13.

52 For more comprehensive discussions of possible accommodations, see Psychiatric Disabilities, *supra* note 18, and Adam A. Milani, *Disabled Students in Higher Education: Administrative and Judicial Enforcement of Disability Law, supra* note 19.

53 Wynne v. Tufts Univ. Sch. of Med., 932 F.2d 19, 25 (1st Cir. 1999).

54 Letter to Bates College (Me.), No. 01-96-2053 (Office of Civil Rights Region I 1997) (criticizing college for not having procedures for ensuring that faculty received proper notice of the needs of students with disabilities); *see generally* N.J. Institute of Technology, Counseling Center, *Working with Students with Disabilities: Information for Faculty*, http://www.njit.edu/publicinfo/pdf/counseling_ada2004.pdf (2004).

55 28 C.F.R. § 35.134(b) (2006); 34 C.F.R. § 104.61.

56 The web site for the Educational Testing Service Network is http://www.ets.org. *See also* Psychiatric Disabilities, *supra* note 18, at ch. 2.

57 DePaul Univ. (Ill.), Complaint No. 05-89-2029, 1993 NDLR (LRP) LEXIS 1107, at **30–31; 4 NDLR (LRP) 157 (Office of Civil Rights Region V May 18, 1993).

58 20 U.S.C. § 1232g (2000); 34 C.F.R. pt. 99 (2006).

59 42 U.S.C. § 300gg (2000); 29 U.S.C § 1181 (2000); 45 C.F.R. pts. 160, 164 (2006).

60 For more comprehensive treatments of FERPA, consult *The Family Educational Rights and Privacy Act: A Legal Compendium* (Steven J. McDonald ed., 2d ed., 2002), and The Catholic University of America, The Office of General Counsel, *FERPA*, http://counsel.cua.edu/ferpa/clicks/ (last updated Aug. 17, 2004).

61 34 C.F.R. § 99.1.

62 34 C.F.R. § 99.3; U.S. Department of Education, *FERPA: Frequently Asked Questions*, question 7, http://www.ed.gov/policy/gen/guid/fpco/faq.html#q7 (last visited Apr. 29, 2006).

63 34 C.F.R. pt. 99(D).

64 20 U.S.C. § 1232g(a)(4)(A).

65 Melissa Bianchi, The HIPAA Privacy Regulations and Student Health Centers (NACUA 2006).

66 34 C.F.R. § 99.31 (the list above is only a partial list of permitted disclosures). It is important to note that these disclosures are permissive, but not mandatory.

67 34 C.F.R. § 99.36.

68 34 C.F.R. 99.31(a)(14) ("The institution must not disclose the final results of the disciplinary proceeding unless it determines that – (A) The student is an alleged perpetrator of a crime of violence or non-forcible sex offense; and (B) With respect to the allegation made against him or her, the student has committed a violation of the institution's rules or policies").

69   "The disclosure may only include the final results of the disciplinary proceeding conducted by the institution of postsecondary education with respect to that alleged crime or offense. The institution may disclose the final results of the disciplinary proceeding, regardless of whether the institution concluded a violation was committed." 34 C.F.R. § 99.31(a)(13); *see also* 34 C.F.R. § 99.39.

70   34 C.F.R. § 99.36(b)(3).

71   Kline v. Dept. of Health & Human Servs., 927 F.2d 522, 524 (10th Cir. 1991).

72   Gonzaga Univ. v. Doe, 536 U.S. 273, 287 (2002); *see also* Zona v. Clark Univ., ___ F. Supp. 2d ___, 2006 WL 1793627 (D. Mass. June 26, 2006) (university baseball player failed to state a claim for damages against the university or university administrators in connection with a coach's alleged disclosure to the rest of the team that the student suffered from a bipolar disorder; the student asserted claims under the Public Health Service Act, FERPA, and Title III of the ADA).

73   For a more complete discussion of HIPAA and how it relates to colleges and universities, see Pietrina Scaraglino, *Complying with HIPAA: A Guide for the University and Its Counsel*, 29 J.C. & U.L. 525 (2003).

74   45 C.F.R. § 164.500.

75   45 C.F.R. § 160.103.

76   *Id.*

77   *Id.*

78   Universities may also provide employee or student health benefits through group health plans and other arrangements that qualify as HIPAA-covered health plans.

79   The Catholic Univ. of Am., The Office of General Counsel, *Summary of Federal Laws*, http://counsel.cua.edu/fedlaw/HIPAA.cfm (last visited Apr. 29, 2006).

80   Rob Capriccioso, *Confidentiality Preserved at GW*, http://insidehighered. com/news/2006/06/22/waiver (June 22, 2006).

81   *See generally* James Archer, Jr. & Stewart Cooper, Counseling and Mental Health Services on Campus: A Handbook of Contemporary Practices and Challenges 211–13 (1998).

82   *E.g.*, Elissa R. Weitzman, *Poor Mental Health, Depression, and Associations with Alcohol Consumption, Harm, and Abuse in a National Sample of Young Adults in College*, 192 J. Nervous & Mental Disease, Apr. 2004, at 269.

83   Bickel & Lake, *supra* note 2, at ch. VI.

84   Peter F. Lake & Joel C. Epstein, *Modern Liability Rules and Policies Regarding College Student Alcohol Injuries: Reducing High-Risk Alcohol Use Through Norms of Shared Responsibility and Environmental Management*, 53 Okla. L. Rev. 611 (2000).

85   594 A.2d 506 (Del. 1991).

86   601 N.W.2d 757 (Neb. 1999).

87   987 P.2d 300 (Idaho 1999).

88   2003 WL 21524786 (Conn. Super. June 19, 2003).

89   Peter F. Lake, *Private Law Continues to Come to Campus: Rights and Responsibilities Revisited*, 31 J.C. & U.L. 621, 646 (2005).

90   *Id.* at 656–58.

91   William DeJong et al., *Environmental Management: A Comprehensive Strategy for Reducing Alcohol and Other Drug Use on College Campuses*, preface, http://www.edc.org/hec/pubs/enviro-mgnt.html (1998).

92   *Id.*; *see Environmental Management: An Approach to Alcohol and Other Drug Prevention*, Prevention Updates (Newsltr. of the Higher Educ. Ctr. for Alcohol & Other Drug Abuse & Violence Prevention) (July 2002), *available at* www.higheredcenter.org/pubs/prev-updates/em101. pdf (identifying the "Keys to Success" in implementing environmental

management strategies as comprehensive efforts, strong presidential leadership, faculty involvement, staff involvement, student involvement, needs assessment and strategic planning, resources, evaluation, and patience and persistence).

93   DeJong et al., *supra* note 91, at 3–5, 12–30.

94   *See* William DeJong et al., *supra* note 91.

95   The NIM report is available at http://www.iom.edu ?id=15100&redirect=0.

96   The NIAAA reports are available at http://www.collegedrinkingprevention.gov/Reports/.

97   Southern Illinois University Carbondale, *Core Institute*, http://www.siu.edu/departments/coreinst/public_html/ (2006) (select "Surveys").

98   Darby Dickerson & Peter F. Lake, *A Blueprint for Collaborative Risk Management Teams*, 38 Campus Activities Programming, Apr. 2006, at 16.

99   DeJong et al., *supra* note 91; Lake & Epstein, *supra* note 84.

100 Southern Illinois University Carbondale, Core Institute, *Results from 2004 Core Survey*, –http://www.siu.edu/departments/coreinst/public_html/ (select "Results").

101 Bickel & Lake, *supra* note 2, at ch. VI.

102 Peter Lake & Nancy Tribbensee, *The Emerging Crisis of College Student Suicide: Law and Policy Responses to Serious Forms of Self-Inflicted Injury*, 32 Stetson L. Rev. 125, 127 (2002) (citing and discussing Lisa C. Barrios et al., *Suicide Ideation Among U.S. College Students: Associations with Other Injury Risk Behaviors*, 48 J. Am College Health 229 (2000)).

103 *See* Rob Capriccioso, *Self-Injury Epidemic*, http://insidehighered.com/news/2006/06/05/injury (June 5, 2006) (discussing a survey in which "researchers found that about 17 percent of undergraduates

and graduate students report that they have cut, burned, punched or harmed themselves in other ways").

104 Jed Foundation, http://www.jedfoundation.org (2005).

105 Suicide Prevention Resource Center, *Suicide Prevention Basics*, http://www.sprc.org/suicide_prev_basics/youth.asp (last visited Apr. 29, 2006) (select "colleges"); *see also* Elizabeth Fried Ellen, *Suicide Prevention on Campus*, 19 Psychiatric Times, Oct. 2002, at 1, *available at* http://www.psychiatrictimes.com/p021001a.html.

106 Jed Foundation, http://www.jedfoundation.org (2005).

107 Jed Foundation, *Framework for Developing Institutional Protocols for the Acutely Distressed or Suicidal College Student* 4 (2006), *available at* http://www.jedfoundation.org/framework.php.

108 *Id.*

109 Lake & Tribbensee, *supra* note 102, at 126.

110 *Id.* at 130 (discussing McLaughlin v. Sullivan, 461 A.2d 123 (N.H. 1983)).

111 *Id.* at 133.

112 *Id.*

113 *Id.* at 131 (discussing Wallace v. Broyles, 961 S.W.2d 712 (Ark. 1998)).

114 *Id.* at 134.

115 John Higgins, *Degrees of Justice*, Akron Beacon Journal, Mar. 12, 2006, at A1 Metro, *available at* http://www.ohio.com/mld/ohio/news/14080493.htm.

116 Elmer Smith, *The informant, the Lies, the Injustice—And a Life Lost*, Phila. Daily News, Mar. 24, 2006, *available at* http://www.philly.com/mld/dailynews/news/local/14174624.htm.

[117] Lake & Tribbensee, *supra* note 102, at 132–33.

[118] *Id.* at 133.

[119] *Id.* (quoting *McLaughlin*, 461 A.2d at 126 (emphasis in original)).

[120] *Id.* at 135.

[121] *Id.*

[122] 617 N.W.2d 293 (Iowa 2000).

[123] *Id.* at 295–96.

[124] *Id.* at 294, 300. A court may grant a motion for summary judgment when there are no genuine issues of material fact and the party who filed the motion is entitled to judgment as a matter of law. Thus, the grant of a motion for summary judgment is considered a decision on the merits, even though the matter does not proceed to trial.

[125] *Id.* at 297–98.

[126] *Id.* at 300. Another recent case followed the rationale in *Jain* and found that lay college deans did not owe a duty to prevent a student's suicide because they lacked specific knowledge about whether the student was at immediate risk of suicide. Mahoney v. Allegheny College, Memorandum and Order, AD 892-2003 (Ct. Com. Pleas, Crawford County, Pa. Dec. 22, 2005), *available at* http://www.asjaonline.org/attachments/articles/35/Allegheney%20college%20SJ%20decision.pdf.

[127] Schieszler v. Ferrum College, 233 F. Supp. 2d 796, 798 (W.D. Va. 2002).

[128] *Id.*; Schieszler v. Ferrum College, 236 F. Supp. 2d 602, 605 (W.D. Va. 2002).

[129] *Schieszler*, 236 F. Supp. 2d at 605.

[130] *Id.*

[131] *Id.* at 609 (emphasis added).

132 *Id.*

133 *Id.* at 610–11.

134 *Id.* at 612.

135 Lake, *supra* note 89, at 653. In addition to a confidential payment, "[t]he college also agreed to institute a one-time full scholarship with a value of $85,000 in [the student's] name and to modify its policies regarding mental health crisis response on campus." *Student Commits Suicide: Negligent Failure to Intervene: Wrongful Death: Settlement*, Law Reporter, Mar. 2004, *available at* http://www.findarticles.com/p/articles/mi_qa3898/is_200403/ai_n9400033.

136 Civ. Action No. 02-0403 (Mass. Super. Ct. June 27, 2005), *available at* http://www.asjaonline.org/attachments/articles/29/Shin%20v.%20MIT.pdf.

137 Slip op. at 2–8.

138 Slip op. at 8–10.

139 Slip op. at 1, 1 n.1.

140 Slip op. at 15–16.

141 Slip op. at 24.

142 *Id.*

143 Marcella Bombardieri, *Parents Strike Settlement with MIT in Death of Daughter*, Bos. Globe, Apr. 4, 2006, *available at* http://www.boston.com/news/local/articles/2006/04/04/parents_strike_settlement_with_mit_in_death_of_daughter.

144 These cases include a suit against Southeastern Louisiana State by the parents of Courtney Garza, and a suit against MIT by the father of Julia Carpenter. *See generally* Ann H. Franke, *When Students Kill Themselves, Colleges May Get the Blame*, 50 Chron. Higher Educ., June

24, 2004, at B18 (available to subscribers at http://www.chronicle. com/weekly/v50/i42/42b01801.htm).

[145] Boston.com News, *Father Sues Clark over Daughter's Heroin Death*, http:// www.boston.com/news/education/higher/articles/2006/04/10/father_ sues_clark_over_daughters_heroin_death/ (Apr. 10, 2006) (father alleges that daughter's death could have been prevented if the university provided "more student counseling and kept drug dealers off campus").

[146] Lake & Tribbensee, *supra* note 102, at 137.

[147] Joel C. Epstein, *Parental Notification: Fact or Fiction*, http://www.edc. org/hec/pubs/articles/parentalnotification.html (Oct. 6, 1999) (discussing Section 952, Alcohol or Drug Possession Disclosure, of the Higher Education Act).

[148] Barbara Lauren, *MIT Student Suicide Case Settled Out of Court*, AACRAO Transcript, Apr. 5, 2006, *available at* http://www.aacrao. org/transcript/index.cfm?fuseaction=show_view&doc_id=3116).

[149] Jed Foundation, *supra* note 107, at 27.

[150] *Id.*

[151] Lake & Tribbensee, *supra* note 102, at 152.

[152] *Id.*

[153] *Id.*

[154] Nott v. George Washington Univ., No. 05-8503 (D.C. Super. complaint filed Oct. 2005), *available at* http://www.bazelon.org/issues/education/incourt/nott/nottcomplaint.pdf.

[155] *Id. at* 3–4; Susan Kinzie, *GWU Suit Prompts Questions of Liability: School Barred Depressed Student*, Wash. Post, Mar. 10, 2006, at A01, *available at* http://www.washingtonpost.com/wp-dyn/content/article/2006/03/09/ AR2006030902550_pf.html).

[156] *Nott*, No. 05-8503, slip op. at 1–3.

157 *Id.* at 4–5.

158 Ryan Holeywell, *GW Denies Wrongdoing in Case of Who Student Sought Depression Treatment*, George Washington Hatchet, Mar. 9, 2006, *available at* http://www.knowledgeplex.org/news/151966.html.

159 Letter to Marietta College, Complaint No., 15-04-2060, 2005 NDLR (LRP) LEXIS 371, 31 NDLR 23 (Office of Civil Rights Midwestern Div., Cleveland July 26, 2005).

160 *Id.* at **9–12.

161 *Id.* at **6–8 (emphasis added).

162 *Id.* at *12.

163 *Id.* at *13.

164 *Id.* (citing 34 C.F.R. § 104.37). Dismissals and involuntary leaves of absence for students who are severely depressed or suicidal may trigger rights under the ADA, Section 504, local nondiscrimination laws, and university nondiscrimination policies. Accordingly, universities should consider whether a student is disabled under these laws and policies. "If so, compare procedures for involuntary leaves of absence to students with disabilities and students without disabilities." Jed Foundation, *supra* note 107, at 27.

165 *E.g.*, Letter to Bluffton Univ., No. 15-04-2042 (Office of Civil Rights Midwestern Div., Cleveland Dec. 2, 2004), *available at* http://www. nacua.org/meetings/virtualseminars/october2005/Documents/OCR_ BlufftonU.pdf); Guilford College, Complaint No. 11-03-2003, 2003 NDLR (LRP) LEXIS 627, 26 NDLR 113 (Office of Civil Rights Southern Division, North Carolina Mar. 6, 2003).

166 *Suicide Prevention Program Takes a New Approach, Works to Fight Violence Against Self*, Daily Illini, Oct. 7, 2004, *available at* http://www.dailyillini.com/media/storage/paper736/news/2004/10/07/News/; *see also* Rob Capriccioso, *Suicide on the Mind*, http://www.insidehighered.com/news/2006/06/05/acha (June 5, 2006).

[167]   For more information about bullying, see Darby Dickerson, *Cyberbul-lies on Campus*, 37 U. Tol. L. Rev. 51 (2005).

[168]   551 P.2d 334 (Cal. 1976).

[169]   *Id.* at 339–40.

[170]   *Id.* at 345.

[171]   *Id.*

[172]   *Id.* at 340.

[173]   Boynton v. Burglass, 590 So. 2d 446 (Fla. Dist. Ct. App. 1991), *su-perseded by* Fla. Stat. § 456.059; Nassar v. Parker, 455 S.E.2d 502 (Va. 1995), *superseded by* Va. Code Ann. § 54.1-2400.1; *see generally* Peter Lake, *Virginia Is Not Safe for "Lovers": The Virginia Supreme Court Rejects Tarasoff in* Nasser v. Parker, 61 Brook. L. Rev. 1285 (1995).

[174]   449 N.E.2d 331 (Mass. 1983).

[175]   *Id.* at 337.

[176]   *Id.* at 335.

[177]   861 P.2d 768 (Kan. 1993).

[178]   *Id.* at 771–72.

[179]   *Id.* at 780.

[180]   *Id.*

[181]   880 A.2d 357 (Md. 2005).

[182]   *Id.* at 367.

[183]   1999 WL 47153 (N.D.N.Y. Jan. 26, 1999).

184 *Id.* at *7.

185 Estate of Faulkner v. Dixon, No. 06CVS6106 (Wake Co., N.C. Gen. Ct. of Justice, Superior Ct. Div. filed May 17, 2006).

186 Claim for Damages Under Tort Claims Act by Estate of Jessica Lee Faulkner, Filing No. A19561 (N.C. Indus. Commn. filed May 17, 2006).

187 Scott Jaschik, *Inside Higher Ed, Errors of Admission?*, http://www. insidehighered.com/news/2006/05/18/suit (May 18, 2006); Ken Little, *Background Checks Urged for UNC Students*, StarNewsOnline.com, http://www.wilmingtonstar.com/apps/pbcs.dll/article?AID=/20060602/ NEWS/606020370/-1/State%20 (June 2, 2006). For additional information on student criminal background checks, see The Catholic University of America, The Office of General Counsel, *Student Criminal Background Checks*, http://counsel.cua.edu/StudLife/publications//background.cfm (Mar. 10, 2006).

188 E-Mail from Security on Campus, Inc. (June 21, 2006) (referring to Sen. Bill 2002).

189 Samantha Henig, *Chron. Higher Educ.: Today's News, New Law in Virginia Will Require Colleges to Report Applicants' Personal Data to Police*, http://chronicle.com/temp/reprint.php?id=6l515787dzmcc64dfnq2v9 n0m0x2sdf0 (June 21, 2006).

190 *E.g.,* Nova Southeastern Univ., Inc. v. Gross, 758 So. 2d 86, 89–90 (Fla. 2000) (citing cases involving businesses and proclaiming that "[t]here is no reason why a university may act without regard to the consequences of its actions while every other legal entity is charged with acting as a reasonably prudent person would in like or similar circumstances." *Id.* at 90).

191 Dickerson & Lake, *supra* note 98.

192 Univ. of Idaho, Complaint No. 10-98-2009, 1998 NDLR (LRP) LEXIS 470; 13 NDLR (LRP) 127 (Office of Civil Rights Region IX Feb. 24, 1998).

193 St. Thomas Univ. (Fla.), Complaint No. 04-01-2098, 2001 NDLR (LRP) LEXIS 553; 23 NDLR (LRP) 160 (Office of Civil Rights, Southern Div., Atlanta Dec. 19, 2001).

194 Letter to San Antonio College (Tex.), Complaint No., 06-03-2020, 2003 NDLR (LRP) LEXIS 857; 27 NDLR 30 (Office of Civil Rights, Southern Div., Dallas June 27, 2003).

195 Regents of Univ. of Mich. v. Ewing, 474 U.S. 214 (1985); Board of Curators of Univ. of Mo. v. Horowitz, 435 U.S. 78 (1978).

196 Gill v. Franklin Pierce Law Ctr., 899 F. Supp. 850 (D.N.H. 1995).

197 *See supra* Section 3.3.

198 Singh v. George Washington Univ. Sch. Med. & Health Servs., 368 F. Supp. 2d 58 (D.D.C. 2005); Steere v. George Washington Univ. Sch. Med. & Health Servs., 368 F. Supp. 2d 52 (D.D.C. 2005). In subsequent decisions, the court found that neither student had a disability. Singh v. George Washington Univ. Sch. Med. & Health Servs., ___ F. Supp. 2d ___, 2006 WL 1897220 (July 12, 2006); Steere v. George Washington Univ. Sch. Med. & Health Servs., ___ F. Supp. 2d ___, 2006 WL 1897223 (D.D.C. Jul7 12, 2006.

199 Letter to Coastline Cmty. College (Cal.), Complaint No. 09-03-2076, 2003 NDLR (LRP) LEXIS 993; 27 NDLR 223 (Office of Civil Rights, Western Division, San Francisco Aug. 19, 2003).

200 Psychiatric Disabilities, *supra* note 18, at 27.

201 *See generally* United Educators, *Administrative Leave and Other Options for Emotionally Distressed or Suicidal Students*, Risk Research Bulletin: Student Affairs, Apr. 2006, at 1, 3–5 (available to UE subscribers at www.ue.org).

202 Carlin v. Trustees of Bos. Univ., 907 F. Supp. 509, 511 (D. Mass. 1995).

203 666 F.2d 761 (2d Cir. 1981), *superseded by rule as stated in* Zervos v. Verizon N.Y., Inc. 252 F.3d 163 (2d Cir. 2001). For a more in-depth

discussion of *Doe* and related issues, see Gary Pavela, The Dismissal of Students with Mental Disorders (1985).

204 *Doe*, 666 F.2d at 766.

205 *Id.* at 767.

206 *Id.* at 770.

207 *Id.* at 775–77.

208 138 S.W.3d 123 (Ky. 2004).

209 *E.g.*, Cleveland State Univ. (Ohio), Complaint No. 05-92-2102, 1992 NDLR (LRP) LEXIS 1112; 3 NDLR (LRP) 198 (Office of Civil Rights, Region V Sept. 29, 1992).

210 Letter to Regent Univ. 2003 NDLR (LRP) LEXIS 890, 27 NDLR 63 (Office of Civil Rights, S. Region, D.C. (N.C.) Nov. 20, 2003).

211 Cal. State Univ., Complaint No. 09-95-2026, 1995 NDLR (LRP) LEXIS 1799; 7 NDLR (LRP) 96 (Office of Civil Rights, Region IX June 12, 1995).

212 Ferrell v. Howard Univ., 1999 WL 1581759 (D.D.C. Dec. 2, 1999).

213 Because the law generally requires that accommodations be offered in the most integrated setting appropriate to the needs of individuals, the university should take steps to ensure that any options that could be perceived as less than full integration of the re-admitted student were reasonably necessary to meet the twin obligations of accommodation for the student and safety for the campus community.

CHAPTER 4

Key Issues for Faculty Regarding College Student Mental Health

Stephen L. Benton, Sherry A. Benton, and Michael F. Perl

N*ancy was a very intelligent student with high ACT scores. In spite of this, she had no close ties with any faculty members in her college, and her grade point average hovered around 2.0. She attended classes erratically, which caused her to miss assignments and be unprepared for examinations. She had a history of not finishing things she started. She would try to draw attention to herself by dressing outlandishly, dying her hair odd colors, and* *wearing elaborate jewelry and noticeable body piercing. Her clothes were often wrinkled and sometimes stained, and she frequently had irritating body odor. She carried an iPod constantly and fidgeted with it compulsively. It was not until she was dismissed for academic deficiencies that she came into contact with an academic advisor. By then it was too late. Although the advisor worked to help her to be reinstated the following semester, Nancy failed to attend classes and eventually left the college permanently.*

Nancy's instructors probably did not know that she battled depression most of the time but refused to take her medication. What, if anything, might faculty members have done to intervene earlier with Nancy? How prevalent are such mental health disabilities among college students? This chapter addresses these questions and considers what aspects of the faculty/student relationship are relevant to student mental health issues. Other questions discussed are whether instructors are required to make accommodations for students with mental disabilities, how they distinguish between a student with a mental health issue and a student of insufficient competence, and how they might express concern to a student who is dealing with depression or another mental illness.

PREVALENCE AND IMPACT OF COLLEGE STUDENT MENTAL HEALTH PROBLEMS

As several authors in this book have noted, counseling center staff are becoming concerned about increases in mental health problems among college students, problems both perceived (Gallagher, Gill, & Sysco, 2000; Robbins, May, & Corazzini, 1985) and observed (Benton, Robertson, Tseng, Newton, & Benton, 2003). Benton et al. (2003) found across a 13-year period (1989–2002) that students who were seen in recent years frequently had more complex problems that included anxiety and depression. Over the 13-year period, the number of students seen each year with depression doubled.

Such increases are a concern to faculty because mental health problems are associated with lower academic achievement. Researchers at Kansas State University found that mood difficulties explained 25% of the variance in student learning problems and that such difficulties interfered significantly with students' academic functioning (Robertson, Benton, Newton, Downey, Marsh, Benton, Tseng, & Shin, in press). Other researchers have found that, when left untreated, prolonged depression can lead to difficulties in cognitive functioning (Haines, Norris, & Kashy, 1996). Anxiety can also interfere with students' attention and retrieval processes, which hinder how much students absorb during class and recall at test time (Spence, Duric, & Roeder, 1996).

Faculty-Student Relationship

Faculty members must be prepared for the likelihood that a student with a mental health issue could be enrolled in one of their classes. They are in the best position of anyone on campus to observe both students' academic and interpersonal behaviors (Rodolfa, 1987). How faculty members respond to students who are exhibiting problems may affect whether students will succeed academically. However, the hierarchical nature of the faculty-student relationship can sometimes be a hindrance, especially at the graduate level. As the Committee on the College Student Group for the Advancement of Psychiatry (1999) pointed out, faculty can have substantial influence on students' feelings of self-worth:

Professors are in a position to encourage or discourage students by the style and content of their comments. A faculty member can be hurtful in the ordinary course of tutoring or sometimes in the administration of oral qualifying exams. Then it is very difficult for a young person to maintain a sense of self-worth while trying to become a genuine scholar or investigator. As a result, the student may experience a substantial loss in self-confidence, not only because the teacher is realistically endowed with considerable power, but also because of an additional attribution of power by some students who experience teachers as parent substitutes. (p. 40)

To counteract this power issue, faculty and administrators should be more caring in their interactions with students (Beck, 1994). Although Noddings (2005) points out the difficulty in operationally defining caring, most authors emphasize expressing interest, concern, positive regard, and respect (e.g., Gilligan, 1982; Mayeroff, 1971). One way to express a caring attitude is to learn students' names. Instructors can assign seating charts, photograph students, or ask them to place their pictures on a course Web site. Instructors should also create an atmosphere of mutual respect because students are more motivated when they feel accepted in the classroom (Spaulding, 1992). One of the most positive things that can happen to a college student is to develop a personal relationship with an instructor or professor. A positive, personal relationship with only one professor can make a difference in students' intellectual and academic skill development, learning, and interest in an occupation (Pascarella & Terenzini, 2005).

Faculty Legal Responsibilities

Although students with mental health problems do not always struggle academically (Farnsworth, 1957), most faculty members recognize that mental health issues can impede students' academic achievements. In a survey of 113 faculty members at one public university on the East Coast, Backels and Wheeler (2001) found that the majority of respondents believed 14 of 15 mental health issues (e.g., anxiety, stress, substance abuse, depression) could have a significant effect on students' academic performance. However, the majority of respondents would extend flexibility to students in meeting academic obligations for only 6 of the 15 mental health problems. Whereas 78.6% of faculty rated anxiety as having a significant effect on academic performance, only 42.4% would be flexible in allowing students to meet academic obligations. Similarly, although 84.6% perceived depression as a significant detriment to academics, only 64.3% would extend flexibility. So, whereas faculties recognize that student mental health problems can affect achievement, not all instructors are eager to make accommodations.

But what are the legal responsibilities of faculty when it comes to students with mental health disabilities? Relevant federal laws are Section 504 of the Rehabilitation Act of 1973 and the Americans with Disabilities Act (ADA) of 1990, both of which affect colleges and universities. According to ADA, a person with a disability is someone with a physical or mental impairment that substantially limits one or more major life activities. Section 504 stipulates that a person with a disability cannot be denied access to or benefit from an activity provided by any institution receiving federal financial assistance.

So how must faculty members comply with Section 504 and

ADA? First, they must afford students with a mental disability the educational opportunity equal to that of other students. For example, an anxiety disorder can hinder a student from performing optimally in a testing situation. Therefore, a student who would otherwise be competent in a work situation might perform poorly when taking an exam. Instructors must provide accommodations to a student with such a disability who qualifies based on documentation from an appropriate mental health professional or psychiatrist. The student is responsible for providing the documentation, but the college or university is responsible for determining the appropriate accommodation and the services that must be provided. In this case, the instructor could allow the student with an anxiety disorder to take the exam in a different location, free from distractions, and allow him or her periodic breaks to engage in relaxation techniques.

Besides requiring equity and accommodations, ADA also protects the confidentiality of a student's mental health problem. A faculty member who feels concerned about a student such as Nancy might be tempted to ask her whether she has a mental health problem. However, federal law prohibits faculty from asking such questions. In fact, a student seeking accommodations does not even have to inform the faculty member about the exact nature of the disability. The professor might only receive direction from a disabilities services office that certain accommodations must be made, not the reason for the accommodations. That can be frustrating to a faculty member who may question the validity of the accommodation. However, staff within a disabilities services office cannot provide details about the disability unless the student has signed a written consent form. If the student were to inform her instructors about the mental health problem, they would be obligated to maintain confidence about the disclosure.

Faculty members who disagree with the recommended accommodations can express their disagreement to staff at the disabilities services office; however, they are nonetheless obligated to provide the accommodation. Examples of accommodations for mental health issues include, but are not limited to the following: taped lectures, alternative testing arrangements, referral to outside agencies, extended test time, recording devices, and counseling (Tacoma Community College, 2006).

In addition to making accommodations, instructors can do several things to help students with mental health disabilities advocate for themselves. They should put a statement on their syllabi, such as the following:

> If you have any reason, such as a disability, which will make it difficult for you to carry out the work as outlined or which will require academic accommodations, please notify the instructor during the first two weeks of the course so that appropriate arrangements can be made.

Faculty members might also print on their syllabi the location of the disabilities student services office and the counseling center. They could also list institutional resources such as student support services, academic support services, tutoring or mentoring programs, resources for students with disabilities, health services, and wellness programs that can be helpful to students struggling with stress (Harper & Peterson, 2004).

MENTAL HEALTH PROBLEMS VERSUS PROBLEMS OF INSUFFICIENT COMPETENCE

Do Section 504 and ADA mean that faculty must tolerate and pass students who are insufficiently competent to work in their respective fields? The answer is an emphatic "No," because that is absolutely not the intent of the legislation. The challenge for faculty is to distinguish between (a) a mental health problem that, with remediation, would not interfere with professional competence and (b) competence deficits that should prevent someone from working in a professional field. The opening scenario to this chapter describes the former situation, because Nancy clearly had the intellectual and academic potential to have excelled were it not for her debilitating mental health problem. In the following case, however, remediation would not have removed the student's insufficient competencies:

> *Jason was admitted into his college's secondary education social studies program, although he barely met entrance requirements. His grades in English composition, algebra, and biology were mostly C's, D's, and F's. During his second semester of professional education, he struggled with a course in reading across the curriculum because he had a limited understanding of the elements and teaching of reading. He performed poorly in the clinical experience because he was often unprepared to teach and he presented information in a disorganized manner. Eventually, Jason became disillusioned with his career choice, fell into a depression (a condition that had hounded him for the past few years), and wrestled with suicidal thoughts. After a conversation with his clinical supervisor, who recommended that he seek help*

for his depression, he started attending therapy sessions at the university counseling center. The therapy helped him to cope with his depression.

The next semester, Jason began student teaching at a local high school. About two weeks into the semester, his cooperating teacher asked him to read to students from the textbook. He was unable to read fluently to the point that students made fun of him, and they were unable to understand what he was reading. That same week the teacher asked him to grade an objective test of key historical names, dates, and events. He took longer to complete the grading than the teacher expected, and when she looked over the exams she noticed that he had failed to mark incorrect answers on several of the papers. She informed him that he needed to be more careful in grading the next time. The next week, she sat next to him as he graded the papers, and she discovered he was unable to read sufficiently to detect correct and incorrect answers. The following day the cooperating teacher contacted the university supervisor to discuss Jason's progress.

The clinical supervisor, who had referred him to counseling previously, then met with Jason and during the course of the conversation, Jason admitted to having been diagnosed with a learning disability in elementary school. Although he had received assistance during his K–12 career, he had never sought accommodations as a college student. The supervisor then referred Jason to the disabilities services office where staff made suggestions for accommodations. The cooperat-

ing teacher then made several accommodations, including an electronic spell checker, a computer, and extra time for preparing instruction and grading papers. However, Jason failed to make adequate progress and was dismissed from student teaching before the end of the semester. Even with the accommodations, Jason was not sufficiently competent to teach social studies. He graduated with a degree in education but with the understanding that he would not receive a teaching license.

Although the college made several accommodations for Jason's disability, and he received counseling for his mental health problem, the faculty made the decision that he was insufficiently competent to be a classroom teacher. Just because accommodations were made did not mean the college was required to pass a student who was not ready to teach.

RESPONDING TO STUDENTS WITH MENTAL HEALTH PROBLEMS

Jason's clinical supervisor recognized that he had a mental health problem and made the appropriate referral. Although that referral did not solve his problem with teaching competence, it might have prevented him from taking his own life. Key faculty responses when they have a student of concern can be summed up in the "three Rs": *recognize, respond,* and *refer.* Faculty members need to recognize when a student seems to be struggling or exhibiting some symptoms of mental or emotional difficulty. Next, they need to respond to the student by asking questions or expressing concern as in, "I've noticed that…," and then just talk about their concerns. Last, they need to refer the student to appropriate resources such as the counseling center. Frequently, faculty members hesitate to approach the subject of mental or emotional difficulties with students even when signs of a problem are readily apparent. For example, a biology professor once told Sheryl A. Benton, a co-author of this chapter, that she had a lab assistant who seemed to be losing weight so fast that she was "disappearing before her eyes." The faculty member feared that the graduate student had an eating disorder but was afraid she would offend the student if she brought it up and found out she was wrong. In such cases, the faculty member must weigh the risks of offending the student, who might not actually have an eating disorder, or of allowing the student to die if she were truly anorexic. The greater risk is clearly in failing to approach the subject.

Besides practicing the "three Rs," faculty can work within their institutions to create policies and procedures that increase the likelihood that others will recognize, respond, and refer. One example of a successful set of policies and procedures is Kansas State University's "College of Education Qualitative Aspects of Student Performance" (http://coe.k-state.edu/Departments/CSPS/Handbook/StPerform.html). The National Council on Accreditation of Teacher Education (NCATE) recognized the policies and procedures described in this document as exemplary.[1]

The document begins with a statement of its intent:

> This must not be a system to discourage the refreshingly odd or the delightfully uncommon person. We would, rather, aspire to ensure that those with special gifts are not lost to the profession because of the lack of early recognition or encouragement, while at the same time ensuring equally early identification of those about whom there is increasing doubt in regard to the appropriateness

of their choices and judgment. This document describes principles and aspirations we hold for such a monitoring system, principles which should guide the thinking and actions of those of us who have responsibility for supporting and encouraging promising educators, as well as the responsibility for reducing the chances of endorsing persons for whom endorsement would be a mistake. This document also sets out policies and procedures for implementing the system. (p.1)

The document proposes a method of identifying students of special concern—both positive and negative—and of coordinating inquiries and interventions. At the end of each semester, the assistant dean sends all instructors in the college a letter along with a copy of their class roster from the Office of Student and Professional Services. Faculty are asked to simply place a check mark next to the name of any student for whom they have special concerns, either positive or negative. They are also asked to briefly describe the issue of their concern. This procedure ensures that periodic assessments of students are conducted, a hallmark of successful policies (Amada, 1992). When a concern is reported, a faculty committee decides what kind of response is appropriate, within the guidelines of the policies. The most common response would be to contact other persons who have been associated with the student of concern to ascertain whether or not other professionals have similar concerns. As a result of these contacts and discussions, the faculty committee would, with the combined judgment of those acquainted with the student's performance, decide whether or not further action should be taken at that time, and if so, would establish the appropriate procedures, given the conditions of concern. Step-by-step procedures are described that ensure the student's due process rights are protected.

Another example of a program designed for early identification of students with problems is Mississippi State University's (MSU) Pathfinder program. Winner of the Noel-Levitz Retention Excellence Award, Pathfinder identifies first-year students who miss more than two classes in the first six weeks of the semester. Instructors keep track of student attendance and alert student affairs officials of students having potential problems. Pathfinder staff, comprised of student assistants, contact the students via phone, e-mail, or a personal visit to remind them about the importance of class attendance. MSU also pairs incoming first-year students with faculty mentors and staff volunteers who are available to answer questions and provide support. Since Pathfinder's inception, student attendance and retention have increased significantly. Perhaps just as importantly, MSU faculty and staff communicate to parents and students that they want to know if a student is having a problem.

Another action faculty members can take within their departments is to communicate with others when they have a concern about a student. Faculty can access a student's schedule and contact other instructors to see if they also have concerns.

For example, Stephen A. Benton, first author of this chapter, team-teaches an eight-credit-hour block of three courses with two other faculty members. Students in the major must enroll in all three courses simultaneously during the first semester of their junior year. The three faculty members collaborate on planning and teaching so that common themes are embedded across the courses and redundancy is reduced. They also meet weekly to plan classes and to discuss the progress of individual students. Through the years, the weekly meetings have helped to identify students who appear depressed, come to class with alcohol on their breath, appear overly thin, sleep in class, have notice- able body odor, cry easily, are defiant, ask questions incessantly, exhibit declining quality of work, attend erratically, and lack follow-through on assignments. On a few occasions, the team has met with individual students to express concern and, in some cases, to make referrals to the university counseling center or other campus office. On more than one occasion, students have decided not to continue in the major. At other times, they have decided to seek professional help. Most of the time, however, these early interventions have resulted in the students chang- ing their behaviors so that they can complete the eight-hour block successfully.

The lessons learned from this team-teaching experience are many. First, faculty members are more likely to identify a student of con- cern if they talk to others who teach the same student. Most of the time, others share the concerns expressed. Second, there is strength in numbers. Faculty feel empowered to intervene with a student when they have the backing of colleagues. Third, meeting regularly to chat about students helps faculty members remember that they are teaching not just content but students. In this era of recruitment and retention concerns, putting students as a priority makes good business sense.

Finally, faculty should get to know the professional staff at the counseling center and disabilities services office. These individuals can be a tremendous source of support and information to faculty who find themselves angry or fearful about students who are experi- encing mental health problems (Lamb, 1993). For example, faculty might request that a member of the counseling center be present whenever there is a meeting to remove a student from a program.

Another possibility would be to have counseling center personnel review any written policies on retention or removal of students from a program. Faculty could also invite counseling center staff to attend one department meeting each year, to meet for coffee, or to socialize in other informal gatherings.

CONCLUSION

Faculty members are uniquely qualified to assess college students' academic and interpersonal behaviors. By building positive relationships with students, faculty can provide encouragement and make a difference in their lives. All instructors are legally compelled to make accommodations for students who qualify as having a mental health problem and to hold in confidence information about the student's disability. However, students of insufficient competence should not be passed or certified in a program merely because they have a mental health issue. Perhaps what is most important for faculty to remember is to follow the three Rs when dealing with a student of concern: recognize, respond, and refer. Ultimately, faculty members should keep open lines of communication with the student and with colleagues who may share similar concerns.

Footnotes

[1]   "The unit has developed a detailed policy (with examples), and a procedure which makes clear to students and faculty alike the values to which the unit is committed. The practice was identified as exemplary because of the completeness of the rationale, the fullness of the presentation to students and faculty and the existence of an operational procedure to counsel students out of the program when they do not meet program expectations" (NCATE Board of Examiners Report, Kansas State University, March 15–19, 1997).

References

Amada, G. (1992). Coping with the disruptive college student: A practical model. *Journal of American College health, 40*, 203-215.

Backels, K., & Wheeler, I. (2001). Faculty perceptions of mental health issues among college students. *Journal of College Student Development, 42*, 173-176.

Benton, S. A., Robertson, J. M., Tseng, W., Newton, F. B., & Benton, S. L. (2003). Changes in counseling center client problems across thirteen years. *Professional Psychology: Research and Practice, 34*, 66-72.

Committee on the College Student Group for the Advancement of Psychiatry. (1999). *Helping students adapt to graduate school: Making the grade.* New York: The Haworth Press, Inc.

Farnsworth, D. L. (1957). *Mental health in college and university.* Oxford, England: Harvard University Press.

Gallagher, R. P., Gill, A. M., & Sysco, H. M. (2000). *National survey of counseling center directors 2000.* Alexandria, VA: International Association of Counseling Service.

Haines, M. E., Norris, M. P., & Kashy, D. A. (1996). The effects of depressed mood on academic performance in college students. *Journal of College Student Development, 37,* 519-526.

Harper, R. & Peterson, M. (2005). Mental health issues and college students. *NACADA Clearinghouse of Academic Advising Resources.* Retrieved March 20, 2006, from http://www.nacada.ksu.edu/ Clearinghouse/AdvisingIssues/Mental health.htm

Kansas State University College of Education. Qualitative aspects of student performance. Retrieved March 21, 2006, from http://coe.k-state.edu/Departments/CSPS/Handbook/StPer-form.html

Lamb, S. C. (1992). Managing disruptive students: The mental health practitioner as a consultant for faculty and staff. *Journal of College Student Psychotherapy, 7,* 23-39.

Noddings, N. (2005). *The challenge to care in schools: An alternative approach to education* (2nd ed.). New York: Teachers College Press.

Pascarella, E. T., & Terenzini, P. T. (2005). *How college affects students: A third decade of research.* San Francisco: Jossey-Bass.

Robbins, S. B., May, T. M., & Corrazini, J. G. (1985). Perceptions of client needs and counseling center staff roles and functions. *Journal of Counseling Psychology, 32,* 641-644.

Robertson, J. M., Benton, S. L., Newton, F. B., Downey, R. G.,

Marsh, P. A., Benton, S. A., Tseng, W., & Shin, K. (in press). K-State Problem Identification Rating Scale (K-PIRS) for college students. *Measurement and Evaluation in Education.*

Rodolfa, E. R. (1987). Training university faculty to assist emotionally troubled students. *Journal of College Student Personnel, 28,* 183-184.

Spaulding, C. L. (1992). *Motivation in the classroom.* New York: McGraw-Hill.

Spence, S. H., Duric, V., & Roeder, U. (1996). Performance realism in test-anxious students. *Anxiety, Stress, and Coping, 9,* 339-355.

Tacoma Community College. Important information for faculty and staff. Retrieved March 21, 2006 from http://www.tacomacc.edu/resourcesforstudents/counselingandadvisingcenter/accessservices/importantinformationforfacultyandstaff.aspx

CHAPTER 5

Mental Health Consultation for Urgent and Emergent Campus Issues

Fred B. Newton

A rcher and Cooper (1998, pp. 120–121) defined mental health consultation as an activity conducted outside of the counseling or mental health center, where a staff member provides advice and assistance based on psychological principles for a campus constituent (whether it be for a group, office, department, club, or other entity). Consider the following examples of issues that create a need for consultation by a mental health professional:

> **Scenario 1:** A student shows hostility through some form of threat. This problem may present

questions of interpretation about the cause of behaviors, sanctions or mandates for correction, or the relatedness of behaviors to other issues such as harassment or prejudice.

Scenario 2: A student demonstrates some psychological impairment, either diagnosed or evident by symptom behavior, which interferes with an ability to manage personal, social, or academic performance. With this type of problem, faculty and staff must determine how to accommodate a student's right to receive an education within the means and resources made available by the institution. They may also consider whether the student's situation disrupts the educational progress of other students.

Scenario 3: One or more students behave in ways that are disruptive or antithetical to the educational purpose and values of the institution. Examples could be alcohol or drug issues, unusual violence or tensions in social groups, and riotous behavior at athletic events.

Scenario 4: A natural disaster or traumatic event affects a large segment of the campus population. In this situation, administrators must decide how to stabilize the emotional disruption, calm or adjust the aftermath, and consider corrections or adjustments needed for returning to the educational process.

The role of the mental health professional as campus consultant has been discussed in the literature for more than 30 years. The goal of this chapter is to identify several themes for mental health consultation prevalent on college and university campuses today, note the advantages and cautions for using mental health consultation, and finally, to outline suggestions for good practice.

Several forces in higher education today require careful consideration in deciding how a campus might handle a problem situation with mental health implications: the Americans with Disability Act, The Family Education and Rights and Privacy Act (FERPA), and a series of legal precedents when dealing with endangerment issues such as suicide and threat. Because these topics are discussed in a separate chapter of this book, they are mentioned here only as a point of consideration.

MODELS OF PSYCHOLOGICAL CONSULTATION

Models have been developed to demonstrate how psychological consultation may be effective as a campus intervention. Morrill, Oetting, and Hurst (1974) conceptualized consultation as a cube. The cube included three dimensions: the target for consultation (individual, group, or campus as system), the intervention level (prevention, remediation, or developmental), and the delivery method (direct contact, training, consultation, or media). The cube model has been used by many over the years to describe the range and strategies for psychological consultation and outreach.

Caplan's model (1970) has been the classic standard for explaining levels or types of mental health consultation. The first level is the client- or student-centered approach that focuses on a plan to deal with a specific student problem. The consultant helps to assess and diagnose the issue and prescribe a course of action. On the second level, the focus is not on an individual student problem but on how a consultee, such as a professional staff or faculty member, may develop with skills, solutions or strategies to work with a situation. An example might be a department head who must handle a situation where there is conflict and stress between staff members of the department. On the third level, the consultant suggests an approach to improve a program or policy in order to handle an institution-wide concern at an administrative level. An example might be designing an educational or policy intervention to deal with an alcohol-abuse situation in a social club.

Delworth (1989) described the Assessment-Intervention of Student Problems approach (AISP model) to deal with students who are either having problems or causing problems with others on campus. The AISP model generally describes the type of consultation and intervention process that is typical in some form on most college and university campuses today. The model, depicted with a flow chart of action that moves from assessment to intervention, considers three levels: the individual student, the campus systems involved, and the intervention or outcome process. At the individual level the staff members consider the severity of social disturbance. Could the behavior be dangerous to self or others? Is there interference with property or the educational process? The typical campus process may include the judicial system (or an element thereof including judicial affairs, Dean's office, or a reporting authority), the mental health system (designee from a counseling center, mental health agency, or psychological service agency), and the campus intervention team (CIT), which is composed of those with knowledge of or vested interest in the problem. Depending upon the nature of the situation, the CIT could include a variety of staff and faculty representatives (e.g., residence life staff, dean of students, chaplains, attorneys, and department representatives) who provide relevant input or follow-up. The outcome might include a treatment or educational intervention, implementation of a policy or procedure, or a decision that could include student withdrawal, sanctions, or special conditions.

ROLES AND RESPONSIBILITIES OF THE MENTAL HEALTH CONSULTANT

The mental health consultant has specific roles that might change at each of the three stages of the AISP model. The first stage could be labeled the assessment stage. The task in assessment is to provide— through interview, observation, and other means of data collection—an evaluation of the needs, causes, and factors present in the situation. Several communication skills are important for building rapport with a disruptive individual: the ability to explore and listen carefully, to explain and interpret, and sometimes to mediate.

Assessment leads to the second stage where the consultant works with an intervention team of professionals, requesting its input in deciding how to respond. The team assists in making appropriate inferences from the assessment stage and in providing recommendations for potential solutions, remediations, or sanctions. The mental health consultant might also lead a discussion of alternative viewpoints and provide the mental health perspective. However, in some cases, the mental health representative should maintain objectivity in order to remain an agent of remediation at the implementation stage.

During the final stage of implementation, the consultant's role may be that of intervention, education, or instruction. This could include directing or describing options, or serving as a mediator and facilitator for communication of a follow-up to what might be a very sensitive campus concern. When a mental health problem is involved, the consultant may at times prescribe objectives for resolution, (e.g., make a treatment recommendation) and confirm that these objectives have been met.

CONTRIBUTIONS AND LIMITATIONS OF A MENTAL HEALTH CONSULTATION

A few questions clarifying what mental health professionals (psychiatrist, psychologist, social worker, counselor) may or may not offer in consultation might help to dispel some misperceptions and unrealistic expectations.

Can a mental health consultant predict future human behavior? The mental health consultant should not provide definitive predictions about whether the person will act with threat or danger to self or others. The best predictor of future behavior is often past patterns of behavior. Evidence of past behaviors might come from residence hall staff, police, faculty, friends, and family. The mental health professional can provide a piece of this puzzle by describing symptoms and patterns that are characteristics of established mental health diagnoses. By helping to interpret behavioral patterns in the context of personality or mental disorders, the consultant can recommend potential options (e.g., treatment, remediation) for dealing with a problem.

How should a mental health professional be used as part of an involuntary mandate, intervention, or remediation for a student found in violation of a policy? Mental health consultants should exercise caution in deciding the role they play in intervention with or remediation of student problems. For example, a student is likely to view "sentencing" to counseling or treatment as punishment for violation of a policy. This sets up unsatisfactory expectations for open and acceptable remediation of a problem behavior. A better approach would be to contract with the student a responsible self-management approach. If a student violates a behavioral policy, the contract should specify the behavior to be corrected. The student should be responsible for developing a plan to show that he or she understands how to correct the behavior. The counselor or other designated support person may then consult with the student to assess the need for change that will help the student make improvement and complete the contract.

What can a mental health consultant contribute in determining an appropriate response to a disruptive or traumatic event? Maggie Olona (2005), director of counseling at Texas A&M University, indicated that when asked to be the consultant at a time of campus crisis, the best skill to offer is that of a facilitator and process manager. Frequently, when an emergency or critical situation arises there is a sense of urgency for answers or solutions. However, Olona offered that the best initial response is the "stop, look, and listen" approach. Process questions, such as, "What are you concerned about? What are you afraid will happen? What would you like us to do?" help to clarify what is needed. Action is then based on what needs to be done, what can be done, and what additional resources might need to be tapped (Olona, 2005).

WHAT OTHER ISSUES MAY NEED TO BE ADDRESSED WITH AN ON-CAMPUS CONSULTANT?

When a consultant is coming from within the institution, there are several caveats that should be considered. One is the potential conflict that exists with dual roles in a situation. For example, a mental health consultant could be in conflicting roles as a counselor to a student and a consultant to a department on how to deal with a complaint against the student. Obviously a mental health professional must avoid conflicting expectations when roles could overlap. However, through a written release, a student client may request that the counselor make a recommendation on his or her behalf in response to a problem the student is having on campus. In this case, the recommendation is being made from the counselor's role and not as a consultant to the office or department in question. Similarly, a mental health worker acting as a consultant to the institution should not conduct an evaluation of a student's competency if that evaluation could lead to the student's dismissal. In most cases, a consultant outside the institution should complete the evaluation, thereby avoiding the perception that the institution is acting in a self-serving manner.

Should the mental health consultant stay professionally aloof from the rest of the campus or build relationships and connections with as much of the campus personnel as possible? Some mental health professionals believe that maintaining distance from the administration and faculty protects student confidentiality and increases objectivity when making recommendations. Although confidentiality and professional standards should be safeguarded, building relationships with other campus personnel establishes trust and influence. When crises occur and problem situations arise, there is little time to develop such relationships. Longstanding relationships and confidence allow a working alliance to begin immediately following a crisis, with clear understanding of expectations and limitations.

THE AISP MODEL REVISITED

The AISP model (see Figure 5.1), described previously, still has relevance today. The AISP model starts with the *act* or event that is labeled the disturbance, crisis, or problem affecting a student, group or the educational environment. But, prior to any event (this may be noted as phase four in the revised AISP model), most institutions have written a set of established guidelines or policies in anticipation of possible problems that could arise. These policies typically address such problems as sexual harassment, violent or threatening behavior, suicidal behavior, natural disasters, sexual assault, destruction of property, behavior that distracts with educational process, alcohol and drug use, mental health disorders, and so forth. The policies require a commitment to educate campus personnel about detection, violations, and even prevention of the problem. Two very helpful resources in developing policies or protocols are NASPA's book, *Crisis Management: Responding from the Heart* (Harper, Patterson, and Zdziarski, 2006); and The Jed Foundation's "Framework for Developing Institutional Protocols for the Acutely Distressed or Suicidal College Student" (Jed Foundation Web site, 2006).

Phase 2 of the AISP model is the *intervention* team meeting to decide on a course of action. At this point, a number of campus employees must come together to assess the situation and suggest what might be done. Multiple viewpoints ensure that due process, safety, confidentiality, and legal codes are followed. The intervention team might be comprised of attorneys, medical staff, mental health professionals, safety officers, police, deans, department heads, faculty, and relevant support personnel. A student advocate might also be present to ensure due process.

The third phase of the AISP model (*student problem*) reflects the recommended action to be taken. Possibilities include sanctions, mandates, or strictures on the student that might include removal from the institution, a step that considers both the individual rights and protection of the environment. Action might also include steps for assistance, treatment, or education that can provide the correction and support needed for maintenance and success in the educational environment. Any of these actions may be deemed serious to the status of a student and/or the safety of the campus.

The final phase of the revised AISP model demonstrates the *process* of change that creates a continuing cycle based upon evaluation and experience. At this point, evaluation may lead to policy development and the creation of protocols or guidelines to anticipate or direct future problem situations. Experience must lead to reflection and evaluation of future needs that in turn may result in new actions. For example, the Texas A&M University bonfire tragedy, in which 12 students were killed after the traditional bonfire collapsed on them, led to a "responsibility management" policy that specified that any high-risk activity (such as bonfires or driving campus vans) requires training and education about potential dangers and ways to respond. Similar changes are evident when campuses have been confronted with suicides, group alcohol violations, and other episodes that affect campus safety. The ultimate outcome of any disturbing event is a review, evaluation, and determination of what can be done to prevent, respond, or educate in the future. Essentially, the model would have a circular flow that allows for continual improvement of policy, response systems, and preparation of the campus at many levels.

In summary, the best intervention model for responding to behavioral violations and campus crises clearly specifies procedures, protocol, resources, and consultant expertise available. All procedures follow fair and equitable due process. Collaboration and communication among many segments of the campus is essential to a successful resolution.

Such a model allows personnel the flexibility to adapt to unique situations and to change policies and procedures based upon new knowledge and situations.

Figure 5.1. AISP Model Revisited.

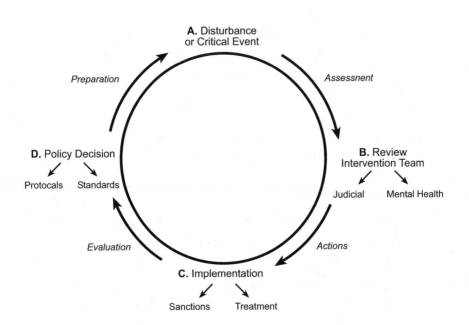

Source: Adapted from Delworth, 1989.

REFERENCES

Archer, J. & Cooper, S. (1998). *Counseling and mental health services on campus: A handbook of contemporary practices and challenges.* San Francisco: Jossey-Bass.

Caplan, G. (1970). *The theory and practice of mental health consultation.* New York: Basic Books.

Delworth, U. (1989). The AISP Model: Assessment-Intervention of Student Problems. In U. Delworth (Ed.), Dealing with the behavioral and psychological problems of students. *New Directions for Student Services, 45,* pp. 3-14. San Francisco: Jossey-Bass.

Harper, K. S., Paterson, B. G., & Zdziarski, E. L. (2006). *Crisis management: Responding from the heart.* Washington, DC: NASPA.

JED Foundation. (2006). Framework for developing institutional protocols for the acutely distressed or suicidal college student http://www.jedfoundation.org/framework.php

Morrill, W. H., Oetting, E. R., & Hurst, J. C. (1974). Dimensions of counselor functioning. *Personnel and Guidance Journal, 52,* 354-359.

Olona, M. (2005). *Mental health professionals as consultants for urgent or emergent student issues.* Paper presented at the annual meeting of the Association of University and College Counseling Center Directors, Minneapolis.

CHAPTER 6

Counseling and Mental Health Services

Stewart E. Cooper

This chapter focuses on the major issues and challenges currently facing college and university counseling centers. Perhaps the first comprehensive examination of this topic was *The Counseling Psychologist* special issue on "College and University Counseling Centers in the 1990's," edited by Stone and Archer (1990). Subsequently, Archer and Cooper (1998) gave these issues significant attention in their book, *Counseling and Mental Health Services on Campus*. Recently, the highly popular book, *College of the Overwhelmed*, by Kadisson (2005), brought national attention to the mental health issues of college students and the pressures these put on often under-funded campus counseling centers.

Current issues and challenges facing college and university mental health centers fall into four thematic domains: (a) the increased demand for counseling center services combined with either steady or decreasing levels in clinical staff sizes, (b) counseling center structural challenges, (c) the professional staff, and (d) issues emerging from the changing legal and ethical environment. Under these four domains, this chapter presents a total of 17 issues.

CHALLENGES AND ISSUES OF THE CLINICAL DEMAND/ PROFESSIONAL STAFF RESOURCES GAP

Issue 1: In the face of increasing severity, complexity, and quantity of mental health cases, counseling center staff have seen zero growth in resources or reduced budgets.

The intersection of increased demand for services without increased personnel resources is having a marked affect on the nature of services provided. The majority of universities have fiscal concerns. The majority of costs for college and university counseling center are for professional and support staff salaries and benefits, which increase every year. Yet, most institutions have experienced reductions in their funds for such non-faculty, non-equipment, and non-building costs. In response to this situation, almost all counseling centers have adopted a brief therapy approach, and many have initiated session limits (either in the number of sessions per year or per lifetime at the institution). Some centers are now charging a fee for services. Keeling and Heitzmann (2003) made a case that generating income to supplement declining college and university general funds is here to stay, particularly at large institutions. Additionally, they outlined an array of funding opportunities that college and university counseling centers might access. Counseling center staff may feel conflicted about the traditionally free service they have provided in the past and the trend toward charging nominal fees. However, most administrators are becoming comfortable with charging students for mental health care (Keeling & Heitzmann, 2003). This trend toward becoming more self-sustaining raises two questions: First, Where does it end? Second, are college and university counseling centers to become cost centers or perhaps even money generators?

Issue 2: Due to a combination of highly publicized litigation and the heightened involvement of many parents, college and university counseling centers are dealing with increasing liabilities and responsibilities for stabilizing students with severe emotional disabilities. Simultaneously, pressure is escalating to assist others who live in close community with such students as well as to reduce risks to the institution in general. The response to the above pressures often involves adding more services to manage the ongoing acting-in or acting-out behavior of the individual.

In cases of severe disturbance, counseling services staff often must provide services to not only those students with significant pathology but also to numerous other students, faculty, and staff. Mental health professionals often have to balance the needs of the individual with those of the various 'communities' with which these students are involved across the institution. Conflicting opinions regarding confidentiality can create inter-staff difficulties. Except in cases of immanent danger to self or others, without an information release, college and university counseling center staff typically cannot break confidentiality to discuss the client with others in the college or university system. This strict code can be frustrating to other student affairs and academic affairs professionals who may believe strongly that free-flowing communication is in the best interest of a particular student.

Issue 3: College and university counseling centers are facing the challenges of incorporating and using newly emerging technologies while simultaneously protecting students' confidentiality.

Today's students have grown up with computers, cell phones, the Internet, and many other communication technologies. They typically possess more advanced technical knowledge and skills than the staff at the counseling center, even those who are current on computer hardware and software technology. Many students check out the Web site of the counseling center (if one is available), and most clients prefer to communicate by e-mail or cell phone. What is interesting is that neither of these latter technologies is very secure. However, conveying this security risk to students seems to make little difference in their preference to use these means of communication and interaction.

Issue 4: Today's students typically work part-time while pursuing a college degree and face pressures to acquire more academic minors and majors and to accrue extracurricular involvements, the combination of which makes it difficult for campus mental health centers to schedule groups.

In the last 10 years or so, the college and university counseling center literature has urged college and university mental health services staff to develop and sustain a viable groups program (Parcover, Dunton, Carter, & Gehlert, 2006). A central tenet of these arguments is that group counseling is a superior means of delivering not only efficient but efficacious clinical services. Furthermore, groups are well-suited to the developmental issues of the young adult clinical population. Groups are efficient because multiple students can receive counseling simultaneously. Groups are efficacious because many issues could be more successfully treated in a group counseling format. Specifically, group counseling typically allows for in-vivo modeling, role playing, and vicarious learning. Nonetheless, many counseling center staffs have found it very difficult to create a viable groups program (Kincade & Kalodner, 2004). Besides students' increased time commitments—from working to earn money for tuition or entertainment to building their resume—many students who are potentially interested in such group experiences have concerns about privacy. This is especially the case on smaller campuses where most students know each other or at least have mutual friends. Compared to individual therapy where confidentiality is assured in all but a handful of extreme situations, these close inter-personal connections can serve as a significant barrier.

Issue 5: The availability of increasingly focused medications for mental health problems, along with more marketing by the pharmaceutical industry, have increased demands for counseling centers to offer combined treatment (i.e., counseling plus medication). This is especially true for arriving students who are already on one or more medications or who have already received counseling and medication earlier in their lives.

In this country, there has been a radical increase in the availability and use of psychotropic medications to alleviate psychological issues

(*Whitaker*, 2005). This is part of the broader influence that the highly powerful and well-resourced pharmaceutical industry is having on the nation. The message is "pills can help and are safe" or perhaps even "the right pill is all that you need." More students than ever are coming to the counseling center already having been on such medications, and more students than ever are seeking such medications to assist with their functioning and/or feelings. The result is a significant pressure to increase the availability level of psychiatrists or psychiatric-nurse practitioners, both of which incur relatively high cost. Yet again, economic resources are usually not provided to college and university counseling centers to cover this growing pressure to provide such services.

Issue 6: Due to the increasing diversity of the student body, accompanied by the need for targeted services and service providers, college and university counseling centers are under increasing pressure to provide culturally informed services to a growingly diverse campus population. Individuals who provide such services must be sensitive to students from a variety of cultures with divergent world views, and who likely favor differing domains of interventions.

Mental health professionals who have graduated in recent years have typically had a strong exposure to multiple aspects of multiculturalism and multicultural counseling (e.g., gender, sex, sexual orientation, race, ethnicity, socio-economic status, religion, culture). Those who graduated prior to the mid-1990s have had to learn about these matters independently. Yet several courses and supervised applied experiences cannot prepare clinical staff for the diversity among clients they will be asked to assist. College and university counseling center directors, especially at larger institutions, may come under significant pressure from various constituency groups to hire new staff members from some particular ethnic or cultural group who might relate best to clients from that same group. More generally, college and university counseling centers are under both external and internal pressure to hire staff members who are from diverse backgrounds or who have a strong commitment to provide culturally informed practice. In fact, this stress on successfully working with diverse cultures in today's psychological treatment environment means that the internal pressures that staff at college and university counseling centers face in their job searches may be stronger than those coming from the outside.

Issue 7: Due to legal and media pressures, counseling centers are facing ongoing pressure to provide specialized services for difficult campus issues such as substance abuse, eating disorders, dating violence, academic failure, and so forth.

High-profile cases in each of the above areas continue to call attention to these issues. Furthermore, each of these clinical issues is likely to harm students' academic performance. College and university counseling centers are expected to provide treatment (to facilitate recovery) and tertiary prevention counseling (to avoid further deterioration) for those whose lives are already adversely affected. Many counseling centers are also expected to offer secondary prevention (targeted to at-risk groups) and primary prevention (to promote mental hygiene) through outreach programs and consultation to head off problems in the above areas. Such educational and prevention work is often valued by many but can be very difficult to deliver if the center's staff resources are inadequate to meet the needs even for direct services. When such a situation exists, the vast majority of mental health units will feel compelled to focus only on treatment.

Issue 8: Due to globalization and other world changes, college and university counseling centers face increased pressure to help students deal with a future that contains much greater job and economic uncertainty and much less safety than students of 10 years ago faced.

Fear and security issues are the bottom level of Maslow's Hierarchy of Needs. It is arguable that the effects of economic globalization and the current armed conflicts in the world—especially 9/11 and the presence of U.S. troops in Iraq and Afghanistan—have significantly increased anxieties about the future among college students. Most students who come for counseling do not focus on these international matters, and most might not even be aware that such global happenings are having an impact on them. Nonetheless, some of the anxiety and depression that students are presenting when they seek intakes at college and university counseling centers is likely to be due to these global factors.

CHALLENGES AND ISSUES RELATED TO STRUCTURING OF SERVICES

Issue 9: Choosing what type of counseling center model to follow that best fits the campus and the needs of the students, (i.e., clinical vs. developmental; short-term and refer out vs. moderate or longer-term care that responds to most student mental health needs; primary focus on individual vs. group therapy; balance of treatment/tertiary prevention vs. secondary prevention vs. primary prevention).

Archer and Cooper (1998) outline six distinct models for campus counseling center structures, depending on the context of the institu-tion and the role that the counseling center is asked to play. These range from a comprehensive counseling, consultation, and community model to a privately contracted clinical sessions model. Especially for those institutions that want a broad range of mental health services, the current growing disparity between level of demand and level of resources is increasing tertiary prevention at the cost of doing less sec-ondary and primary prevention.

Issue 10: College counseling centers face challenges in developing referral networks.

Most college and university counseling centers now refer clients out, either because their professional staff members do not have the expertise or time resources to meet clients' specialized clinical needs or because the clients' mental health issues would best be addressed in a different treatment venue. For many campus mental health centers, referrals are now being made to community providers because a model of short-term therapy is the only service offered by the center. How-ever, regardless of the cause for referral, most centers often don't know how well students are doing once they leave the triage service. Partly because of age and lack of experience in obtaining health care provid-ers, and partly because of the complexity of medical insurance, it is un-likely that many students successfully make this transition. Counseling centers should develop local referral sources and specialized treatment referrals for issues such as substance dependency and severe eating dis-orders. Finally, given the nature of the academic calendar, some clients need assistance and support in locating referral resources within the communities where they are going to reside during major time breaks from the school.

Issue 11: For counseling centers to decide how much direct involvement faculty, staff, and/or students should have in delivering or collaborating on mental health services.

To be more effective, faculty and staff need training in identifying and responding to distressed students. But providing this training takes a great deal of time and energy (e.g., conducting workshops for faculty or residential assistants to help them communicate with distressed students). Beyond the time and energy for training, significant additional time is also needed to provide ongoing consultation, especially for challenging cases.

Issue 12: Deciding the nature and level of resources to put into counseling center and student mental health evaluation and research activities.

College and university counseling centers, as with most other units on campus, are under increasing pressure to provide accountability for positive results. D. Heitzmann (personal communication, April 8, 2006) noted that for many years, college and university counseling centers have gotten along with what might be considered fairly shaky renderings of collected data. Specifically, data from the main two national surveys comes from counseling center directors' subjective reports, and although some directors provide accurate data, others may offer rough estimates. Using technology now available (i.e., Titanium Scheduler/Data Management Program), the field of college mental health will soon have the ability to accurately and routinely describe and evaluate the state of affairs on a national level, as measured by standardized data. This capacity will result in real time, up-to-date, accurate information and will create a repository for the largest data set ever created on college student mental health. If enough college and university counseling centers adopt common intake systems, outcome measures, and so forth, the field should be able to speak with confidence and authority on the state of mental health among its student constituency.

ISSUES RELATED TO COUNSELING CENTER STAFF

Issue 13: Responding to counselor burnout.

In some cases, professional staff members feel overwhelmed because of the increased demand not only of clinical cases but also for meeting campus needs for programs, consultations, committees, and increased paperwork at every level. Being stretched thin and being expected to do more with less can be leading contributors to this burnout. Another factor is "compassion fatigue," which may be more prevalent among those who have been in the field for a long time (Corey, 2001). Burnout can also come from the demands clients make on therapists and the sense of responsibility therapists feel toward their clients. The data indicate that if one sits with an anxious person, one leaves the session more anxious. Burnout can also come from feeling an inequity on staff, that not all are pulling their weight. And burnout can be fed by staff members chronically questioning the work of other staff members.

Issue 14: Dealing with the issue of low salaries and lack of career advancement opportunities.

Starting salaries for college and university counseling center staff are relatively low and increase slowly, which means they fall farther behind other professional salaries. There are often significant discrepancies between the salaries new employees in college and university counseling centers receive and new faculty members receive, even when those in the counseling center setting are employed for more months during the year. Also, there is a significant absence of career ladders for counseling center staff. This issue particularly plagues mid-level and senior staff because they realize that there are few career advancement opportunities save for the few coordinator or assistant director positions.

Issue 15: Providing training and development for those going into administrative roles.

Attention needs to be paid to the development of counseling center administrators. The Elements of Excellence Task Force of the Association for University and College Counseling Center Directors (AUCCCD) is attempting to do this through the Administrative Institute, but participation typically occurs after someone becomes a director. The college and university counseling center field does not have much in the form of professional development for a staff member aspiring to roles such as training director, associate director, or center director. One recently published book by Herr, Heitzmann, and Rayman (2006), *The Professional Counselor as Administrator: Perspectives on Leadership and Management in Counseling Services,* focuses on this topic and offers a number of ideas about it.

CHALLENGES DUE TO THE CHANGING LEGAL AND ETHICAL CONTEXT

Issue 16: Increasing fears of litigation.

The recent attention to the MIT suicide case and the even more recent attention to the issue of dismissing students for psychological reasons both illustrate the power that fear of litigation has on campus administrators. Such fears affect the counseling center's daily life in that more time is allocated to creating, completing, and storing documentation, and there are changes to many other aspects of service. Also, more time and money are likely to be spent on consultations with campus legal counsels. The most common goals of such consultations are to understand the implications of particular issues for the campus, along with any steps to be taken or not to be taken to lessen these risks.

Issue 17: Increasing regulatory control over actions clinical staff must take to obtain and maintain professional certification or licensure.

College and university counseling centers often have to change procedures or practices in responding to the pressures from professional organizations and state laws that determine certification of licensure and what staff at college and university counseling centers must do in order to qualify for these. In turn, the pressure that student affairs leaders face to have staff members licensed to practice independently come both from legal liability and from various accreditation bodies (e.g., the Association of Psychology Post-Doctoral and Internship Centers (APPIC) that governs internships). Having licensed professionals may reduce institutional liability.

CONCLUSIONS

College and university mental health centers face several major challenges.

1. Demand for counseling center services is increasing but clinical staff sizes are either static or decreasing. Counseling centers, student affairs divisions, and universities in general face difficult choices in determining the scope of services offered and finding the economic resources needed to fund a sufficient level of professional and support staff to deliver these services.

2. Pressures exist to provide time intensive individual and group therapy services, but students can benefit significantly if there are sufficient resources for the staff to provide indirect and community-oriented services. Far more students can be assisted by these consultation and collaboration efforts.

3. Increasing job pressures without increasing support is a formula for job stress and burnout. Universities must address this issue if they are to obtain the longer-term commitment from non-faculty staff that would better serve students.

4. The changing legal and ethical environment continues to expand and to demand response from counseling center staff and student affairs administrators. Planning to provide the resources and support for such an increase would seem a helpful step.

In sum, given the above 17 challenges and issues, college and university counseling center staff and administrators and student affairs leaders face a good deal of complexity in the 21st century. The rapidly changing context of higher education is adding to this mix. Effective response will require creativity and flexibility, plus an influx of resources. A number of resources to assist in doing this are available including a very sharing international network among counseling centers and some new sources of funds such as the Garrett Lee Smith Act.

REFERENCES

Archer, J., & Cooper, S. E. (1998). *Counseling and mental health services on campus.* San Francisco: Jossey-Bass.

Corey, G. (2001). *Theory and practice of counseling and psychotherapy (sixth ed.).* Pacific Grove, CA: Brooks/Cole.

Herr, E. L., Heitzmann, D., & Rayman, J. R. (2006). *The Professional Counselor as Administrator: Perspectives on Leadership and Management in Counseling Services.* Mahwah, NJ: Lawrence Erlbaum Associates.

Keeling, R. P., & Heitzmann, D. (Fall 2003). Financing health and counseling services. *New Directions for Student Services, 103,* 39-58.

Kincade, E. A., & Kalodner, C. R. (2004). The use of groups in college and university counseling centers. In J. L. DeLucia-Waack, D. A. Gerrity, C. R. Kalodner, and M. T. Riva (Eds.), Handbook of group counseling and psychotherapy (pp. 366-377). Thousand Oaks, CA: Sage Publications Ltd.

Parcover, J. A., Dunton, E. C., & Gehlert, K. M. (2006). Getting the most from group counseling in college counseling centers. *Journal for Specialists in Group Work, 31*(1), 37-49.

Stone, G. L., & Archer, J. (1990). College and university counseling centers in the 1990s: Challenges and limits. *Counseling Psychologist, 18*(4), 539-607.

Whitaker, R. (2005). Anatomy of an Epidemic: Psychiatric Drugs and the Astonishing Rise of Mental Illness in America. *Ethical Human Psychology and Psychiatry, 7*(1), 23-35.

CHAPTER 7

Support Services for Students with Mental Health Disabilities

Kenneth J. Osfield and Reynol Junco

The number of college students with psychological disorders has increased steadily over the last decade (University of Wales–Bangor, (n.d.); Hart, 2001; National Mental Health Association, 2005; Royal College of Psychiatrists, 2003: Hobbs, 2003; DeNoon, 2003; Iles, 2003; Curtis, 2003; HERO, 2003; O'Connor, 2001;Young, 2003; Eudaly, n.d.; Locke & Heitzmann, 2005). The American College Health Association conducts a survey for its National College Health Assessment (NCAH) to evaluate health trends on campus, including changes in the numbers of psychological disorders. NCAH findings (see Figure 7.1) show that the percentage of students who reported depression and anxiety in "the last school year" increased steadily from 2000 to 2005 (ACHA, 2005a). Furthermore, 45.7% of the students in NCAH Spring 2005 sample (made up of 54,111 college students) reported being so depressed that they found it difficult to function (ACHA, 2005b). Therefore, it is important for colleges and universities to have support services in place for students with mental health concerns. Because students with psychological disorders are covered under the Americans with Disabilities Act, a key element in the provision of support services is the disability resource office.

Figure 7.1. Increase in % of Students Reporting Mental Health Issues.

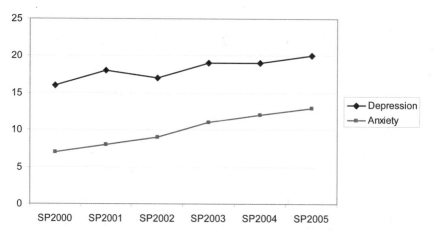

Note. The increase in the percentage of students (SP) who report depression or anxiety in the previous school year.

Source: American College Health Association. American College Health Association–National College Health Assessment (ACHA–NCHA) Web Summary. Updated September 2005. Available at http://www.acha.org/projects_programs/ncha_sampledata.cfm. 2005.

This chapter (a) provides an overview of federal legislation that mandates the provision of services to students with psychological disorders, (b) reviews the more common psychological disorders students on college and university campuses experience, (c) recommends policies and procedures for disability service provision, (d) describes the interface between the counseling center and the disability resource office, and (e) provides referral information for faculty and student affairs professionals.

DEFINITION OF A DISABILITY BASED ON THE AMERICANS WITH DISABILITIES ACT OF 1990 AND SECTION 504 OF THE REHABILITATION ACT OF 1973

Two pieces of federal legislation provide protections for students with disabilities in institutions of higher education. Congress passed the Americans with Disabilities Act (ADA; 1990) and Section 504 of the Rehabilitation Act of 1973 to integrate individuals with disabilities into mainstream society and to prevent discrimination based on whether a person has a disability. The Rehabilitation Act made discriminating against a person with a disability illegal. The Americans with Disabilities Act reinforced the anti-discrimination provisions in the Rehabilitation Act and also required institutions that receive federal funding to make reasonable accommodations for an otherwise qualified person with a disability for all programs, facilities, and services.

The ADA defines a disability as any physical or mental impairment that limits one or more major life activities (learning is classified as a major life activity). A reasonable accommodation is defined as any modification that allows individuals with disabilities equal access to benefits available to individuals without disabilities (for instance, providing books in Braille format is a reasonable accommodation for a student who is blind). Finally, an "otherwise qualified" person is one who meets the essential requirements of the program or service (for example, a student with a disability who enters college must meet the same admissions requirements as other students).

MENTAL HEALTH CATEGORIES

The *Diagnostic and Statistical Manual of Mental Disorders* (DSM-IV) is the standard guide used to categorize and diagnose psychological disorders. The DSM-IV is exceptionally broad in the inclusion of disorders as "psychological disorders." For instance, autism and what are typically referred to as "learning disabilities" fall under the umbrella category of "mental disorders." For the purposes of this chapter, psychological disorders are those that are listed in the DSM-IV, with the exception of learning disabilities (such as reading and writing disorder) and attention deficit hyperactivity disorder (ADHD) because college and university personnel often categorize these disorders as "learning disabilities." Although students with psychological disabilities exhibit a wide variety of psychological disorders, higher education professionals would most likely interact with students that have the following, common psychological disorders:

Anxiety disorders

Panic Disorder Without Agoraphobia – Symptoms include recurrent panic attacks that are characterized by a sudden onset of acute fear accompanied by physiological symptoms such as racing heart rate, difficulty breathing, and/or chest pains. Panic disorder can be extremely restrictive in that a student may want to avoid situations that have brought about panic attacks. One of the more common panic attack triggers for college students is an examination. Although the panic attack may not be directly related to the exam, the stressfulness of the exam environment can increase the likelihood of a panic attack.

Obsessive-Compulsive Disorder (OCD) – OCD is characterized by either obsessions (anxious thoughts that are experienced as intrusive) or compulsions (repetitive behaviors in which one engages to minimize obsessions and reduce anxiety). Students with mild to moderate OCD may find themselves at odds with their roommates, especially when the student engages in compulsions. Some compulsions (like having to knock on the door ten times before stepping outside) can seem like "lunacy" to the student's roommate and to residence hall professionals.

Posttraumatic Stress Disorder (PTSD) – Involves symptoms that are developed after exposure to an acute traumatic event. The event is then relived (much like a flashback) causing a great deal of anxiety. Furthermore, individuals with PTSD attempt to avoid stimuli that remind them of or are associated with the original traumatic event. Generally, the defining PTSD event is something that happened to the student before he or she arrived on campus. As with other anxiety disorders, the frequency and severity of the student's symptoms will increase as other stressors in the environment increase. Sometimes, students with PTSD engage in many avoidance behaviors that may even generalize to not speaking with others or not coming out of their room.

Generalized Anxiety Disorder (GAD) – Is characterized by excessive worry and anxiety that typically lasts for at least six months and that cannot be traced to a specific event. Although GAD is often less severe than the other anxiety disorders listed, the academic and social effects are just as agonizing. Students with GAD may always seem on edge, and they can often be exceptionally worried about their class performance.

Mood Disorders

Major Depressive Disorder – Is distinguished by at least one episode characterized by a minimum period of two weeks of depressed mood or loss of interest in conjunction with other symptoms that include significant weight loss or gain, insomnia or hypersomnia, difficulty concentrating, fatigue, restlessness or decrease in motor responses, and/or recurrent thoughts of death. One or more cognitive deficits are common to see in students diagnosed with depression: difficulty concentrating, confusion, difficulty following directions, and communication problems.

Bipolar I Disorder – Is differentiated from Bipolar II Disorder by the frequency of the person's Major Depressive and Manic Episodes. In a Manic Episode, the person shows an abnormally expansive or irritable mood. People who experience a Manic Episode often feel like they can accomplish many things and feel "pressed" to do great feats. They usually end up taking risks they would not otherwise take. A person diagnosed with Bipolar I has one or more Manic Episodes that are sometimes accompanied by Major Depressive Episodes.

Bipolar II Disorder – Is diagnosed when a person has one or more Major Depressive Episodes accompanied by at least one Hypomanic Episode (a Manic Episode that is less severe in duration and intensity).

Disorders Usually First Diagnosed in Infancy, Childhood, or Adolescence

Autistic Disorder – In the movie "Rain Man," Dustin Hoffman plays the role of Ray, a person with Autistic Disorder. Ray exhibits some of the typical qualities of Autistic Disorder, which include impairment in social interactions, impairment in communication, and repetitive and stereotyped behaviors ("gotta watch Wopner"). College students with Autistic Disorder are usually higher functioning in terms of their academic skills. Although they may seem socially awkward, these students often retain and express a great deal of information about academic topics.

Asperger's Disorder – Colleges and universities have seen a striking increase in the number of matriculated students diagnosed with Asperger's Disorder. The symptoms of Asperger's Disorder are almost identical to those of Autistic Disorder, with the notable lack of impairment in communications. Recent research has suggested that Austistic Disorder and Asperger's Disorder lay along a continuum instead of being discrete disorders. As of late, it is common to hear disability resource professionals describe someone with a high-or low-functioning Autism Spectrum Disorder (Tanguay, 2004). Higher-functioning students within the Autism Spectrum Disorders may show more of an orientation toward people and may seem less socially awkward than someone who is lower functioning.

Personality Disorder

There are a number of specific personality disorders (that include borderline, histrionic, and narcissistic personality disorder). Personality disorders are persistent patterns of behaviors or experiences that deviate significantly from the expectations of the person's culture. Because these patterns are generally inflexible, students with Personality Disorders experience a wide range of symptoms (e.g., Major Depressive Episodes and Anxiety

Disorders) due to their inability to adapt to environmental and cultural expectations. Personality disorders are typically first diagnosed in early adulthood, but college and university counseling center personnel are often the first to recognize them (DSM-IV, 1994).

The main symptoms of most of the abovementioned psychological disabilities directly affect students' ability succeed in their academic work. For instance, if students are depressed, they may show signs of cognitive and processing difficulties. They may have greater trouble following directions for assignments, or they may have trouble remembering something their resident assistant asked them to do. Given the "invisible" nature of these disabilities, those around the student may make negative assumptions based on their interpretation of what is going on (e.g., "Nancy sure seems careless lately—maybe she doesn't want to be in school anymore"). Faculty and staff who do not know about the student's psychological issues may engage in a type of "fundamental attribution error," whereby they attribute the student's behavior to a fault in character and not to a process that may be unrelated to the student's personality makeup (Ross, 1977). Therefore, faculty and staff should learn about and understand the signs and symptoms of psychological disorders. Informational training in this area can create positive attitudes about students with psychological disabilities, and these attitudes can be related to the students' persistence in college (Junco & Salter, 2005). The disability resource office can lead the way in providing training to college or university faculty and staff.

Faculty and student affairs staff also need information about when it is appropriate to make a referral to the counseling center or to the disability resource office. For example, the Centre for Students with

Disabilities at Niagra College (Mental, n.d.) lists indicators of psychological disorders that may signal higher education professionals to make a referral. Some of these signs are:

* Marked personality change over time

* Confused thinking, grandiose ideas

* Prolonged feelings of depression or apathy

* Feelings of extreme highs and lows

* Heightened anxieties, fears of anger or suspicion; blaming others

* Social withdrawal, increased self-centeredness

* Denial of obvious problems and strong resistance to offers of help

* Substance abuse

* Thinking about suicide

If faculty or staff observe any of these indicators, they should refer students to the appropriate office on campus. Either the counseling center or the disability resource office will perform a screening and/or assessment to prescribe the best course of treatment. If accommodations are necessary for the student to function academically, the disability resource office will become involved.

PROVIDING EFFECTIVE AND REASONABLE ACCOMMODATIONS

In order to facilitate referrals to the disability resource office, policies and procedures should be in place so that students are clear about how to obtain accommodations. Through their disability resource offices, colleges and universities should have established policies and procedures for the review of disability documentation and the provision of accommodations. A typical process would be as follows:

1. The student schedules an appointment with the disability resource office or forwards documentation of his/her disability. The student is responsible for identifying the disability to the resource office; however, the institution is responsible for informing students about the process to follow in order to obtain accommodations. College or university staff can communicate the resources available and the procedures students should follow in several ways: at orientation, through academic affairs (such as accommodation statements in syllabi), or through student affairs (such as through RA trainings or residence hall postings).

2. A disability resource professional reviews the documentation to ensure that it follows the institution's established documentation guidelines. The Association on Higher Education and Disability (AHEAD, 2006)

publishes recommended documentation guidelines. For students with psychological disorders, documentation includes the credentials of the evaluator, a DSM-IV diagnosis, full results of psychometric testing or the diagnostic methods used to arrive at the diagnosis, student history and relevant background information, the stability of the disorder, the student's functional limitations, and recommendations for reasonable accommodations.

3. A disability resource professional meets with the student to discuss reasonable accommodations based on the student's strengths and weaknesses. The disability resource professional also assesses whether a referral to a psychologist or a psychiatrist is necessary for continuing care for the student.

4. For classroom accommodations, the disabilities resource office gives students an accommodation letter to provide to their professors. The letter includes biographical information about the student and the accommodations that must be provided. The letter also includes disability resource contact information in case there is a question or concern about the student or the accommodations.

As mentioned in Step 1, colleges and universities must make a reasonable effort to inform students of the services available. For instance, the University of Florida notifies all incoming students about the services available through several channels: the admissions office, new student orientation, various campus publications (student guide, faculty guide, pamphlets) and state-wide publications (state university resource guide and community college resource guide), syllabus statements, and the university Web site. Lock Haven University of Pennsylvania provides all students information about disability services through the admissions office, orientation programs, syllabi statements, and the university's Web site. The following is an example of a syllabus statement:

> Students with disabilities are encouraged to discuss requests for reasonable accommodations with the professor at the beginning of the semester. In order for accommodations to be provided, your disability must be verified by the disability resource office located in 100 Smith Hall, (305) 555-2982, disres@youruniv.edu.

THE ROLE OF THE DISABILITY RESOURCE OFFICE

The college or university is responsible to uphold the provisions of the Americans with Disabilities Act and Section 504 of the Rehabilitation Act. Most universities give the disability resource office the task of coordinating accommodations for students. The disability resource office has a number of responsibilities to ensure that students with disabilities are afforded their legal rights. The staff there is responsible for interpreting federal disability legislation and case law, which shape how disability services are provided.

The disability resource office should be the central campus location where disability documentation is reviewed and stored. Just as medical information is protected under the privacy rule of the Health Insurance Portability and Accountability Act of 1996 (HIPAA), disability information is considered confidential and may not be disclosed without the written consent of the student. Therefore, disability resource offices should have procedures in place to protect student confidentiality. These procedures should include a "release of information" form that a student signs to allow disability resource staff to communicate with appropriate college or university faculty and staff when necessary. The release of information form should clearly state the limitations of confidentiality and how information is typically used. The student may nullify the permission to release information at any time.

The disability resource office serves as a central hub of communication with a student's psychologist or psychiatrist, the counseling center, and academic and student affairs. Sometimes, the disability resource office must also act as an interface with campus health and safety departments, as in the case of students who exhibit marked behavioral and social problems. In such situations, confidentiality is not guaranteed. The disability resource office is legally required to release pertinent information if a student is in clear and present danger of harming him or herself or others, if a student is involved in child abuse or neglect, or if a court presents an order to release information.

Staff in the disability resource office should establish a formalized and effective line of communication with staff in the counseling center, because both groups typically work with a large number of students with psychological disorders. At Lock Haven University, the director of disability services is affiliated with the counseling center and often attends clinical staffing meetings to discuss students shared by both offices. With strong collaboration between the two offices, the services to the student can be seamless, with the disability resource office addressing academic issues and the counseling center providing ongoing treatment.

CONCLUSION

Faculty and student affairs professionals are often unaware of the impact that psychological disorders can have on their students. Psychological disorders, by definition, are invisible to those who are not involved in the student's ongoing care. The disability resource office can provide accommodations to help students with psychological disorders succeed in the necessary social and academic domains of college. Moreover, the disability resource office can support students by educating faculty and student affairs staff about students with psychological disorders. For example, a faculty member recently contacted one of the authors and reported that he was extremely happy to have been informed in advance about a student with Asperger's Disorder enrolled in his class. Given this information, the faculty member read about Asperger's and understood what to expect. When the student expressed frustration about an upcoming exam by talking out loud and wringing his hands during class, the professor was able to handle the situation effectively. Furthermore, the faculty member contacted the disability resource office afterward in order to obtain feedback about the event. This kind of partnership benefits students with psychological disorders and minimizes the stigma attached to such disorders.

Faculty and staff are encouraged to work with all students. When a student requests an accommodation through the appropriate campus agency, staff and faculty should contact the disability resource office immediately. This is especially important when an individual has never requested accommodations. To be proactive, staff and faculty should get to know the disability resource staff on their campus and the specific procedures for providing accommodations. The disability resource staff cannot possibly reach out to all campus staff on their own.

In most cases, students with disabilities do not create extra work for faculty or staff. In the rare instances when extra time is necessary, faculty and staff should contact the disability resource office to discuss the situation. They should also contact the disability resource office when they have concerns about a student, even if that student has not self-identified. Keeping lines of communications open between faculty, staff, and the disability resource office helps to minimize potential problems.

As professionals in the area of disability support, the authors have found an incredible amount of satisfaction when they have seen students with disabilities succeed. Students are more likely to succeed when they have the support of the faculty, staff, and administrators. Students with disabilities are not asking for any favors. All they ask is for equal and fair treatment and, most importantly, equal access to education. By providing appropriate accommodations, faculty and student affairs professionals can create an environment that is relatively free of barriers to the success for students with disabilities.

REFERENCES

AHEAD. (2006). Ahead best practices: Disability documentation in higher education. Retrieved January 29, 2006, from http://www.ahead.org/resources/bestpracticeselements.htm

American College Health Association. (2005a). American College Health Association National College Health Assessment (ACHA-NCHA) Web Summary. Updated September 2005. Available at http://www.acha.org/projects_programs/ncha_sampledata.cfm. 2005

American College Health Association. (2005b). American College Health Association–National College Health Assessment: Reference Group Executive Summary Spring 2005. Baltimore: American College Health Association.

American Psychiatric Association. (1994). Diagnostic and Statistical Manual of Mental Disorders: DSM-IV. Washington, DC: American Psychiatric Association.

Curtis, P. (2003, October 16). One in four students suffer mental illness, psychiatrists say. *Guardian Unlimited*. Retrieved December 21, 2005, from http://education.guardian.co.uk/students/health/story/0,12731,1063595,00.html

DeNoon, D. (2003, February 5). College mental health woes on the rise. *WebMD Medical News*. Retrieved December 21, 2005, from http://aolsvc.health.webmd.aol.com/content/article/60/67089.htm

Eudaly, J. (n.d.). *A rising tide: Students with psychiatric disabilities seek services in record numbers*. GW HEATH Resource Center. Retrieved January 11, 2006, from http://www.heath.gwu.edu/PDFs/Psychiatric%20Disabilities.pdf

Hart, P. (2001, December). Counseling center grapples with increasing numbers of students with serious mental health issues. *University Times, 34*(8). Retrieved December 21, 2005, from http://www.pitt.edu/utimes/issues/34/011206/09.html

HERO. (2003). *A sane agenda*. Retrieved December 21, 2005, from http://www.hero.ac.uk/uk/inside_he/archives/2003/a_sane_agenda5482.cfm?view=print

Hobbs, M. (2003). *The mental health of students in higher education – a report and developmental perspective*. Keynote address at the Staying Well-Practice and Policy National Symposium on Mental Health. Abstract retrieved December 21, 2005, from http://www.tcd.ie/student_counseling/mh/prog.php

Junco, R., & Salter, D. (2005). Improving the campus climate for students with disabilities through the use of online training. *NASPA Journal, 41*(2). Retrieved February 22, 2006, from http://publications.naspa.org/naspajournal/vol41/iss2/art4/

Locke, B., & Heitzmann, D. (2005). *Center for the study of college student mental health*. Retrieved December 22, 2005, from Penn State University Counseling and Psychological Services Web site: http://www.sa.psu.edu/caps/pdf/cscsmh_draft_proposal_10-19-2005.pdf

Iles, A. (2003, November). More students seek help for mental health problems. *Student BMJ, 11*, 399. Retrieved December 22, 2005, from http://studentbmj.com

Mental health disabilities: Overview and definition. (n.d.). Retrieved December 21, 2005, from Niagra College Canada, Centre for Students with Disabilities Web site: http://www.niagarac.on.ca/studying/cswd/mental_health_ovr.htm

National Mental Health Association. (2005). *Campaign for America's mental health: Our challenge.* Retrieved December 21, 2005, from http://www.nmha.org/camh/challenge.cfm

O'Connor, E. M. (2001, September). Student mental health: Secondary education no more. *Monitor in Psychology 32*(8). Retrieved December 22, 2005, from http://www.apa.org/monitor/sep01/stumental.html

Ross, L. (1977). The intuitive psychologist and his shortcomings: Distortions in the attribution process. In L. Berkowitz (Ed.), *Advances in experimental social psychology* (vol. 10, pp. 173-220). New York: Academic Press.

Royal College of Psychiatrists, London. (2003, January). *The mental health of students in higher education.* Retrieved January 12, 2006, from http://www.rcpsych.ac.uk?publications/cr/council/cr112.pdf

Tanguay, P. (2004), Commentary: Categorical versus spectrum approaches to classification in Pervasive Developmental Disorders. *Journal of the American Academy of Child & Adolescent Psychiatry, 43*(2), 181-182.

University of Wales, Bangor. (n.d.). *The mental health guide for students*. Retrieved December 22, 2005, from the University of Wales, Student Services Centre Web site: http://www.bangor. ac.uk/ar/main/ssc/mh_guide.htm

Young, J. R. (2003, February 14). Prozac campus. *The Chronicle of Higher Education*, A37.

CHAPTER 8

Contributing to College Student Mental Health Through Health Promotion and Clinical Health Services

Karen S. Moses

In recent years, there has been increased attention to the relationship between health and learning among college students. Faculty and staff often observe the negative impact on attendance and academic achievement that results when students are tired, sick, hung over, depressed, or worried. College students report that a variety of health conditions and behaviors impede academic performance, and surveys confirm that students with fewer health risk behaviors tend to have greater academic success (Hanson, Austin, and Lee-Bayha, 2004). Student affairs professionals are charged with supporting the learning mission. Therefore it is within the scope of work of student affairs to provide programs and services, develop policies and practices, create campus environments, and lead initiatives that support the health and well-being of the student body. An effective plan to enhance the health and well-being of college students will incorporate health promotion and prevention strategies in addition to ensuring that students have access to clinical health services and counseling. This chapter describes a framework with which to address and enhance the health and well-being of college students, with attention to both health promotion and clinical health services.

RATIONALE TO ADDRESS HEALTH IN HIGHER EDUCATION

In order to discuss the rationale for implementing services to enhance students' health and well-being, it is important to start with working definitions of health and wellness and an understanding of the relationship between these and the academic mission. *Leadership for a Healthy Campus* (National Association of Student Personnel Administrators, 2004) describes health as the "presence of well-being and dignity in the lives of individuals, communities, and cultures. It is the holistic integration of the six dimensions of wellness: physical, emotional, intellectual, social, spiritual, and environmental." The preamble to the Constitution of the World Health Organization (World Health Organization, 1946) defines health as a state of complete physical, mental and social well-being and not merely the absence of disease or infirmity. The WHO recognizes that a person's health is instrumental in his or her ability to lead a socially and economically productive life, which leads to the objective of "attainment by all peoples of the highest possible level of health." The National Wellness Institute (2006) defines wellness as an active process through which people become aware of, and make choices toward, a more successful existence. These definitions explain health and wellness as multidimensional processes that go beyond the absence of disease or infirmity to include the integration of physical, emotional, social, mental, spiritual, and environmental domains, and affect one's ability to lead a productive and successful life.

In the context of higher education, it is important to understand that health influences academic success. The American College Health Association conducts an annual nationwide survey that provides information about the relationship between health conditions and academic performance (American College Health Association, 2006). College student respondents to the spring 2005 ACHA–National College Health Assessment (n=54,111) reported top health impediments to academic performance as stress (32%), having a cold, sore throat or the flu (27%), sleep difficulties (25%), concern for a troubled friend or family member (18%), relationship difficulties (16%), depression or anxiety (16%), Internet use and computer games (14%), sinus infections (9%); death of a friend or family member (8%), and alcohol use (8%). While physical illness and injury impede academic performance, the most common health-related academic impediments reported by students primarily represent social, mental, emotional, and spiritual domains. Critical health-risk behavior areas affecting college students today include alcohol, tobacco, and other drug use prevention; sexual assault, relationship violence and violence prevention; injury prevention and safety; mental health, stress, depression, and suicide prevention; sexual relationships and prevention of unintended pregnancy, sexually transmitted infections, and HIV/AIDS; dietary behaviors and nutrition; and physical activity and fitness (American College Health Association, 2006, 2002).

Negative health behavior can result in negative learning outcomes, and positive health behavior can result in positive learning outcomes. Research on the influence of health on student learning in grades K–12 provides evidence that nutrition affects attention span, general achievement, and motivation (Benton and Roberts, 1988; Pollitt, Lewis, Garza and Schulman, 1982; Schoenthaler, Amos, Dorza, Kelly, and Wakefield, 1991; Schoenthaler, Bier, Young, Nichols and Jansenns, 2000; Simeon and Granthan-McGregor, 1989; Hanson et al., 2004; Murphy et al., 1998). Physical activity programs in schools have been shown to decrease involvement in disruptive behaviors in the classrooms, increase concentration, and improve test scores in math, reading, and writing (Hanson et al., 2004; Sallis et al., 1999; Shephard, 1997; Symons, Cinelli, Janes, and Groff, 1997). Tobacco, alcohol, and other drug use disrupts student learning. Student users have a higher rate of absenteeism, lower grades, reduced attention span, lower motivation, and more negative attitudes toward school (Braggio, Pishkin, Gameros and Brooks, 1993; Dozier and Barnes, 1997; Eggert and Herting, 1993; Ellickson, Saner and McGuigan, 1997; Hu and Keeler, 1998). They demonstrate a decreased sense of well-being, engage in more frequent risk taking behavior, and tend to hold less commitment to conventional values. Students exposed to violence demonstrate a lack of interest in school, behavior problems, absenteeism, and higher dropout rates, and they are more likely to be destructive to property (Bowen and Bowen, 1999; Leitman, Binns, and Duffett, 1995; Bowen, Richman, Brester, and Bowen, 1998; Hanson et al., 2004). Recognition of the relationship between health risk behaviors and academic achievement among youth in K–12 has produced the coordinated school health model used in elementary, middle and high schools throughout the nation in an effort to contribute to the academic achievement of our nation's youth.

AN EFFECTIVE MODEL FOR HEALTH IN HIGHER EDUCATION

Recognizing that health influences the capacity for learning is an important step toward supporting students' health. It is also important that student affairs professionals understand that health is influenced by individual, societal, and environmental factors. Students bring personal attributes that influence their well-being, such as health beliefs, health status, genetics, ethnicity or race, gender, sexual orientation, and other internal influences. In addition, the campus environment and culture can support or impede health. Health behavior and health conditions are, in a sense, communal. Alcohol, tobacco, and drug use; violence; depression; stress; and unsafe sexual behavior impact the student population as a whole. For example, students who do not use alcohol report their sleep or studies are interrupted by students who do (Wechsler, Lee, Kuo, and Lee, 2000); and students report their academic performance is harmed by concerns for their family or friends (American College Health Association, 2006). Student affairs professionals respond daily to a growing number of health and risk behaviors that affect not only the individual student but also the broader campus community. By effectively addressing health and risky behavior—from prevention and education through intervention and enforcement—student affairs professionals will effectively enhance the academic potential of the affected student and the student community. Healthy students need healthy campus communities to support healthy behavior, and vice versa.

The public health model presents a framework for developing a campus health program that is community based, not only focused on the individual. A campus-based public health program provides a comprehensive approach to protect and promote the health of the individual student and the student community as a whole, including sanitary and environmental services, health promotion and prevention services, and treatment and rehabilitation services (Tulchinsky & Varavikova, 2000). An effective campus-based public health program will embrace the principles of public health and develop policies and practices that reflect those principles. Effective campus-based health programs that are grounded on the public health model will:

1. Provide a continuum of programs and services ranging from prevention through treatment.

2. Focus on maintaining the health and well-being of the student population, with special attention to high-risk behaviors.

3. Recognize that health is influenced by multiple factors, including individual, societal, and environmental factors.

4. Recognize that community health impacts individual health.

5. Empower students, faculty, and staff to participate in developing a healthy campus, and in making informed decisions about their own health behaviors.

6. Recognize the influence of social conditions on the health and well-being of specific populations.

7. Understand that positive health outcomes at the population level require complex, integrated plans that will impact health over time.

A campus-based public health approach provides a comprehensive and integrated plan for a healthy campus, including (a) prevention and wellness programs to help students learn to better manage stress, relationships, and sexual situations and to develop self-care routines for sleep, nutrition, and fitness that can support learning; (b) recreational and fitness programs to provide opportunities to engage in physical activity; (c) clinical health services to provide medical care and preventive services for illness and injury; and (d) counseling services to diagnose and treat mental conditions and substance abuse. The rest of this chapter describes a framework for effective health promotion services and for effective clinical health services, as components of a comprehensive campus-based public health approach

Effective Health Promotion Services

Health promotion has been defined as, "Any planned combination of educational, political, environmental, regulatory, or organizational mechanisms that support actions and conditions of living conducive to health of individuals, groups and communities" (American Association for Health Education, 2001). Health promotion services are sometimes called wellness or prevention services, in that the programs and services are designed to support student wellness, and/or prevent negative health outcomes. Health promotion programs and services can be designed to (a) support a healthy lifestyle that reduces susceptibility or exposure to health problems (primary prevention), (b) identify and prevent progress of a condition or behavior and its recurrence (secondary prevention), and (c) to alleviate the negative effects of illness and injury (tertiary prevention) (American Association for Health Education, 2001).

Health promotion services range in size and scope of work depending on campus enrollment, institutional commitment to wellness and prevention, and organizational structure. A small campus may have one health promotion professional or may assign health promotion responsibilities to a clinical practitioner such as a nurse. Campuses with large student enrollment will typically have a small staff of three to five health educators, assisted by technical staff, support staff and students. In the past, health promotion services have most often been embedded in the campus health service. However, it is becoming more common to position health promotion services as a unique department that contributes to the vision and planning within student affairs (Moses, Garner, Wirag, Mart, and Lux, 2006).

In contrast to clinical health services that are focused primarily on diagnosis and treatment of illness and injury, health promotion services often provide primary prevention and secondary prevention programs. It is significant to note that the Council for the Advancement of Standards in Higher Education distinguishes health promotion services from clinical health services, describing clinical health services as an auxiliary service and health promotion services as a campus life service (Council for the Advancement of Standards in Higher Education [CAS], 2006). The CAS (2006) further defines health promotion services as "...prevention, education, and wellness policies and initiatives designed to advance the health of students and the campus community in an effort to enhance student learning and create a strong learning environment. Health promotion serves the learning mission of the institution by enhancing students' capability to be effective, engaged learners, by creating healthy, supportive living-learning environments and by advocating for more socially just campus communities in which every student regardless of identity or background is given equitable access to available learning opportunities." Thus, health and health promotion are broadly defined by the CAS, providing opportunity for student affairs professionals to re-think how health promotion services are defined and delivered on campus.

The CAS (2006) Health Promotion Services Standards are based on the Standards of Practice for Health Promotion in Higher Education developed by the American College Health Association (American College Health Association, 2005). The Standards serve as guidelines for enhancing the quality of health promotion programs in institutions of higher education, recognizing the multidisciplinary background of professionals who work to advance the health of students and campus communities. The Standards emphasize integration with the learning mission, collaboration, cultural competence, theory- and evidence-based practice, and professional development and service. A premise of the Standards is that effective health promotion efforts on college and university campuses include both individual and environmental approaches designed to reduce the risk of individual illness and injury, help students build individual capacity, and address larger institutional issues, community factors, and public policies that shape the health-related decisions that students make.

The CAS (2006) and ACHA Standards of Practice for Health Promotion In Higher Education (2005) recognize that leadership for a healthy campus frequently includes health educators; nurses; physi-

cians; counselors; faculty; and staff from residence life, student activities, campus recreation, orientation, and other student affairs departments, as well as students themselves. These people lead or collaborate
on health promotion and wellness initiatives that advance student
learning and the mission of higher education. Although campus professionals from many disciplines contribute to the health of students,
health promotion professionals should have advanced degrees and
relevant experience in health education, public health, higher education, community development, and other appropriate disciplines (CAS,
2006). Programs and policies surrounding issues such as alcohol and
other drug use, interpersonal violence, sexual health, and mental health
are increasingly viewed as campus-wide concerns that affect student
success, retention, and academic progress. Thus, health promotion
professionals must be capable of providing leadership in planning,
implementing, and evaluating evidence-based strategies designed to accomplish the mission and goals of the institution in collaboration with
other units.

Critical physical, behavioral, and mental health issues affect many
aspects of campus life, and recognition of this has led to a change on
some campuses in the organizational placement of health promotion.
Recognizing the need for health promotion to transcend traditional
programs, expand to address mental and behavioral health issues, and
plan from an integrated campus-wide perspective, many campus health
promotion services are being moved from within the health center to a
more visible position within student affairs. Positioning health promotion as a director-level department can facilitate richer integration of
health promotion strategies across student affairs and across campus
(Moses et al., 2006).

Effective health promotion efforts include a planning process that starts with problem identification and analysis (Glanz, Rimer and Lewis, 2002). The American College Health Association–National College Health Assessment (2006) is a survey instrument that can be used to examine students' health behaviors, experiences and perceptions on a broad range of the most relevant health topics. Other relevant data sources include campus health, counseling, judicial, campus crime statistics, and survey and focus group data that enhance understanding of critical health behavior and interest areas. Health promotion services commonly address such focus areas as alcohol and other drug abuse prevention, sexual violence prevention, sexual health enhancement, nutrition and body image enhancement, obesity prevention, stress management, depression, and suicide prevention. Once critical issues have been identified, it is important for the planning team to determine what is causing the problem and what goals and strategies are likely to result in the best outcomes. Therefore, the planning team must maintain a good working knowledge of current research and trends. It is important to develop an evaluation plan before implementing the program plan in order to evaluate outcomes and improve the program.

A useful framework for campus health promotion planning is the socio-ecological model, which recognizes that campus health and safety are shaped through multiple levels of influence—individual, group, institutional, and community—as well as public policy and societal factors. National leaders in prevention recognize that educational programs targeting individual behavior, when implemented alone, do not adequately affect behavior change. To address health and safety, the campus and community environment must be an important part of the plan. *Leadership for a Healthy Campus* (National Association of Student Personnel Administrators, 2004) provides a user-friendly process and tools for developing plans using the socio-ecological approach. Environmental management offers a similar model to the socio-ecological approach. Information and tools supporting an environmental management approach are available through the U.S. Department of Education Higher Education Center for Alcohol and Other Drug Abuse and Violence Prevention (2006).

Many programs and departments within a given campus contribute to the health and safety of the students. These efforts can be more effective when consolidated into a comprehensive campus plan based on the socio-ecological framework. Specific strategies to influence individual and collective outcomes for the critical health and behavior issues prevalent among college students must be identified in the planning process. Health promotion plans based on the socio-ecological framework or the environmental management approach:

1. Address multiple levels of influence on health-related behavior.

2. Use strategies to change campus culture, such as social norms campaigns.

3. Provide and promote healthy activities and products.

4. Identify at-risk students and direct them to appropriate services and assistance.

5. Implement and consistently enforce policies, with increased severity of penalties for violations. Educate the student community about policies, laws, and consequences.

6. Educate the student community about policies, laws, and consequences.

7. Create and enforce standards for advertising on campus.

8. Develop effective collaborations and coalitions and form strong partnerships with academic and student affairs, students, parents, and the surrounding community.

9. Integrate proactive prevention across departmental lines.

10. Work with the surrounding community to change community culture and enforcement of laws (such as drinking laws).

Campus-based health promotion services are most effective within the context of a comprehensive, integrated campus plan, based on the public health model that monitors health and health behavior trends, develops policies to address environmental influences on health and wellness, and provides assurance that important policies, programs and services will be monitored and continued with utmost quality. Such a plan maximizes the potential for successful health promotion efforts that contribute to the academic and personal success of college students.

Effective Clinical Health Services

Clinical health services support the institutional mission by advancing the health of college students through convenient and affordable medical care. According to the Council for the Advancement of Standards in Higher Education (JCAS,2006), ensuring access to quality clinical health services is an important aspect of creating a healthy campus. Clinical health services are frequently called Student Health Services or Campus Health Services; however, this chapter will use the name given by the CAS of "clinical health services" to discuss the medical services provided for students on college and university campuses.

The scope of clinical health services varies depending on enrollment, number of students living on campus, availability of convenient and affordable services in the local community, as well as other factors. Some clinical health services offer a comprehensive range of medical and auxiliary services including general medicine and specialist appointments; urgent care; triage and referral; laboratory and radiology; pharmacy; medical insurance; immunization; complementary or alternative health services, such as acupuncture, physical therapy, and nutritional counseling; counseling and psychiatric services; environmental health and safety; and support for campus research efforts. Others offer a smaller range of services or provide arrangements for health insurance and/or medical care in community facilities. Clinical health services also work with campus and community prevention programs to manage communicable diseases and address other public health needs on campus.

It is important that clinical health service staff have a good understanding of the relationship between physical and mental health conditions, as students who have experienced assault, intimate partner violence, physical symptoms of anxiety and distress, mental health conditions, eating disorders, and other conditions or trauma may turn first to medical care for assistance. Thus, it is also critical that clinical and counseling services develop and maintain an effective working relationship and referral mechanisms to ensure that students receive the care they need.

The American College Health Association publication, *Guidelines for a College Health Program* (American College Health Association, 1999), describes key elements of effective clinical health services on a college or university campus. These guidelines have been adapted from accreditation manuals produced by the Accreditation Association for Ambulatory Health Care and the Joint Commission on Accreditation of Healthcare Organizations. Clinical health services are governed by standards that are defined by accreditation organizations, laws and professional standards, and licensure and credentialing. It is critical that clinical health services comply with and exceed the expectations of regulating authorities for all services rendered and all professional groups represented on the staff. While it is not required by law, many college-based clinical health services choose to become accredited, demonstrating that the comprehensive range of services provided meets the standards of professional practice.

Regardless of clinic size, effective clinical health services will attend to issues of quality, confidentiality, and cost. Health care delivery should be provided according to professional standards of practice and ethical conduct, with meaningful mechanisms for peer review, risk management, evaluation, and response to outcomes and data trends. Technological advancements allow for online communication with patients, Web-based appointment scheduling, and paperless, electronic medical records. With these advancements come the responsibility to

ensure secure e-communications, Web documents, and record keeping
to protect patient privacy and confidentiality and to maintain compliance with the Health Insurance Portability and Accountability Act
(HIPAA). Effective management of health records and communications requires consultation with legal counsel and campus information
technology services.

The cost of health care in the United States continues to esca-
late. In 2004, health care spending in the United States reached $1.9
trillion and was projected to reach $2.9 trillion in 2009 (Borger et al.,
2006). Campus-based clinical health services can play an important
role in the lives of college students by providing access to affordable
health care, particularly for those students who lack health insurance.
However, providing access to affordable, comprehensive health insurance coverage is an important function of the campus health program,
whether or not the campus offers clinical health services. Health insurance protects students from incurring excessive debt should they experience catastrophic illness or injury. Health insurance should include
coverage for mental health services as well as medical care. Medical and
behavioral health care debt can pose a significant threat to a student's
financial stability, creating a barrier to completion of educational goals.

Clinical prevention services will be a part of an effective clinical
health service. Clinical prevention services are the "medical procedures,
tests or counseling that health professionals deliver in a clinical setting
to prevent disease and promote health, as opposed to interventions
that respond to patient symptoms or complaints" (Partnership for Prevention, 1999). Clinical prevention services on a college or university
campus may include immunization; screening for early identification of
health conditions, such as high blood pressure, diabetes, cervical can-
cer, and sexually transmitted infections; and health behavior screening

and brief intervention for tobacco and alcohol use. Such services help to prevent the spread of infection, improve treatment outcomes, and help students to maintain good health.

Clinical health services may provide patient education services or brief intervention for substance abuse. Patient education services provide instruction for treatment protocols or lifestyle changes to support better outcomes for patients with chronic or lifestyle-related health conditions, such as diabetes, asthma, and obesity. Brief intervention is an effective model to reduce high risk drinking behaviors among college students (Institute of Medicine, 1990; Baer, Kivlahan, Blume, McKnight and Marlatt, 2001; Helmkamp et al., 2003). Brief intervention by health care providers is also recommended in reducing tobacco use (U.S. Public Health Service, 2000). Health care providers who are trained to ask about student alcohol and tobacco use behaviors and respond with brief intervention can contribute to the reduction of high-risk drinking and tobacco use among students. In most cases, the goal of brief intervention is reduced use rather than abstinence. Both brief intervention and patient education can be provided by medical staff, health educators, dietitians, and those who have appropriate training and experience in motivating patients to make significant life change.

Wellness, health, and counseling concerns that affect the lives and academic success of students are multidimensional, requiring attention to primary, secondary, and tertiary prevention as well as treatment; individual, group, and environmental influences on health and behavior; and a multidisciplinary approach. Thus, clinical health services should be integrated as a part of the overall public health model for the campus, along with counseling services, health promotion, and other relevant services.

Conclusion

The evidence that health and wellness contribute to academic achievement cannot be ignored by student affairs professionals, whose responsibility it is to support the academic success of college and university students. To advance the health of students, student affairs professionals must move beyond the traditional thinking that individuals are responsible for maintaining their own good health and that health care is primarily related to the diagnosis and treatment of physical illness and injury. Student affairs professionals must recognize the effect of the environment and the social context on individual health and well-being and implement strategies that protect and promote the health and well-being of the individual student and the student community as a whole. The public health model is an effective approach with which to create a comprehensive and integrated plan for a healthy campus, including prevention and wellness programs, recreational and fitness programs, clinical health services, and counseling services. Student affairs professionals and administrators must provide the necessary leadership to create and implement such a plan.

REFERENCES

American College Health Association. (2006). American College Health Association–National College Health Assessment Web Summary. Retrieved June 2006, from http://www.acha.org/projects_programs/ncha_sampledata.cfm

American College Health Association. (1999). *Guidelines for a College Health Program.* Baltimore: American College Health Association.

American College Health Association. (2005). *Standards of Practice for Health Promotion in Higher Education, Second Edition.* Retrieved June 2006, from http://www.acha.org/info_resources/SPHPHE_statement.pdf

American College Health Association Task Force on National Health Objectives for 2010. (2002). *Healthy Campus 2010: Making it Happen.* Baltimore, MD: ACHA.

Baer, J. S., Kivlahan, D. R., Blume, A. W., McKnight, P., & Marlatt, G. A. (2001). Brief intervention for heavy-drinking college students: 4-year follow-up and natural history. *American Journal of Public Health, 91*(8), 1310-1316.

Benton, D., & Roberts, G. (1988). Effects of vitamin and mineral supplementation on intelligence of a sample of school children. *The Lancet, 1(8578),* 140-143.

Borger, C., Smith, S., Truffer, C., Keehan, S., Sisko, A., Poisal, J., et al. (2006). Health spending projections through 2015: Changes on the horizon. Health Affairs 25, 2, 61W-73W. Retrieved June 2006, from http://content.healthaffairs.org

Bowen, G. L., Richamn, J. M., Brester, A., & Bowen, N. K. (1998). Sense of school coherence, perceptions of danger at school, and teacher support among youth at risk of school failure. *Child & Adolescent Socialwork Journal, 15,* 273-286.

Bowen, N. K., & Bowen, G. L. (1999). Effects of crime and violence in neighborhoods and schools on the school behavior and performance of adolescents. *Journal of Adolescent Research, 14*(3), 319-342.

Braggio, J. T., Pishkin, V., Gameros, T. A., & Brooks, D. L. (1993). Academic achievement and adolescent alcohol abuse. *Journal of Clinical Psychology, 49,* 282-291.

Council for the Advancement of Standards in Higher Education. (2006). *The Book of Professional Standards for Higher Education 2006, 6ᵗʰ Edition.* Washington, DC: Council for the Advancement of Standards in Higher Education.

Dozier, A. L., & Barnes, M. J. (1997). Ethnicity, drug use status and academic performance. *Adolescence, 32*(128), 825-827.

Eggert, L. L., & Herting, J. R. (1993). Drug involvement among potential dropouts and "typical" youth. *Journal of Drug Education, 23*(1), 31-55.

Ellickson, P., Saner, H., & McGuigan, K. (1997). Profiles of violent youth: Substance use and other concurrent problems. *American Journal of Public Health, 87*(6), 985-991.

Glanz, K., Rimer, B. K., & Lewis, F. M. (Eds.). (2002). *Health behavior and health education: Theory, research and practice. Third Edition.* San Francisco: Jossey-Bass.

Hanson, T. L., Austin, G., & Lee-Bayha, J. (2004). *How are student health risks & resilience related to the academic progress of schools?* San Francisco, CA: WestEd.

Helmkamp, J. C., Hungerford, D. W., Williams, J. M., Manely, W. G., Furbee, P. M., Horn, K. A., & Pollock, D. A. (2003). Screening and brief intervention for alcohol problems among college students treated in a university hospital emergency department. *Journal of American College Health, 52*(1), 7-16.

Hu, T., & Keeler, T. (1998). Teenage smoking, attempts to quit, and school performance. *American Journal of Public Health, 88*(6), 940-943.

Institute of Medicine. (1990). *Broadening the Base of Treatment for Alcohol Problems.* Washington, DC: National Academy Press.

Leitman, R., Binns, K., & Duffett, A. (1995). *Between hope and fear: Teens speak out on crime and the community.* New York: Louis Harris and Associates, Inc.

Moses, K. S., Garner, M., Wirag, J. R., Mart, S., & Lux, S. (2006, June). *Expanding Potential Through Position: Emerging Trends for the Organizational Placement of Health Promotion in Higher Education.* Presentation at the American College Health Association Annual Meeting, New York City, NY.

Murphy, J. M., Pagano, M. D., Nachmani, J., Sperling, P., Kane,

S., & Kleinman, R. D. (1998). The relationship of school breakfast to psychological and academic functioning. *Archives of Pediatrics and Adolescent Medicine, 152,* 899-906.

National Association of Student Personnel Administrators. *Leadership for a healthy campus: An ecological approach for student success.* (2004). Washington, DC: National Association of Student Personnel Administrators.

National Wellness Institute. (2006). *Defining Wellness.* Retrieved June 2006, from http://www.nationalwellness.org

Partnership for Prevention. (1999). *Why invest in disease prevention? Results from the William M. Mercer/Partnership for Prevention Survey of Employer Sponsored Plans.* Washington, DC: Partnership for Prevention.

Pollitt, E., Lewis, N., Garza, C., & Schulman, R. J. (1982). Fasting and cognitive function. *Journal of Psychiatric Research, 17,* 169-174.

American Association for Health Education. (2001). Report of the 2000 Joint Committee on Health Education and Promotion Terminology. *American Journal of Health Education. 32*(2), 89-104.

Sallis, J. F., McKenzie, T. L., Kolody, B., Lewis, M., Marshall, S., & Rosengard, P. (1999). Effects of health-related physical education on academic achievement: Project SPARK. *Research Quarterly for Exercise and Sport, 70*(2), 127-134

Schoenthaler, S. J., Amos, S. P., Dorza, W. E., Kelly, M. A., &

Wakefield, J. (1991). Controlled trial of vitamin-mineral supplementation on intelligence and brain function. *Personal and Individual Differences, 12,* 343-350.

Schoenthaler, S. J., Bier, I. D., Young, K., Nichols, D., & Jansenns, S. (2000). The effect of vitamin-mineral supplementation on the intelligence of American school children: A randomized double-blind placebo-controlled trial. *Journal of Alternative and Complementary Medicine, 6,* 19-29.

Shephard, R. (1997). Curricular physical activity and academic performance. *Pediatric Exercise Science, 9,* 113-126.

Simeon, D. T., & Granthan-McGregor, S. (1989). Effects of missing breakfast on the cognitive functions of school children of differing nutritional status. *American Journal of Clinical Nutrition, 49,* 646-653.

World Health Organization. (1946). *Constitution of the World Health Organization.* Retrieved June 2006, from http://whqlibdoc.who.int/hist/official_records/constitution.pdf

Symons, C. W., Cinelli, B., Janes, T., & Groff, P. (1997). Bridging student health risks and academic achievement through comprehensive school health programs. *Journal of School Health, 67*(6), 220-227.

Tulchinsky, T. H., & Varavikova, E. A. (2000). *The new public health.* San Diego: Academic Press.

U.S. Department of Education Higher Education Center for Alcohol and Other Drug Abuse and Violence Prevention. *Environ-*

mental Management: A Comprehensive Strategy for Reducing Alcohol and Other Drug Use on College Campuses. Retrieved June 2006, from http://www.edc.org/hec/framework

U.S. Public Health Service. (2000). *Treating tobacco use and dependence—A systems approach. A guide for health care administrators, insurers, managed care organizations, and purchasers.* Retrieved June 2006, from http://www.surgeongeneral.gov/tobacco/systems.htm

Wechsler, H., Lee, J. E., Kuo, M., & Lee, H. (2000). College binge drinking in the 1990s: A continuing problem. Results of the Harvard School of Public Health 1999 College Alcohol Study. *Journal of American College Health, 48*(3), 199-210.

CHAPTER 9

College Student Mental Health and Special Populations: Diversity on Campus

Megan E. Brent, Jennifer A. Erickson Cornish, Adrienne Leslie-Toogood, Lavita I. Nadkarni, and Barry A. Schreier

Diversity on college and university campuses in the United States may be characterized in many ways. A wide range of ideas, theories, and approaches clearly contribute to a flourishing campus community. Equally importantly, a diverse student population provides rich opportunities for faculty, staff, and students to learn about functioning in an increasingly global society. Students are diverse in many ways including age, ethnicity and race, disability, gender identity, international status, rural/urban

issues, sex and gender, sexual orientation, social class, and spiri-
tuality/ religion. Although student athletes may often be viewed
as privileged, they too comprise a special population facing many
unique challenges. This chapter focuses on four diverse student
populations: domestic students of color; gay/lesbian/ bisexual/ trans-
gender/queer students; international students, and student-athletes.

Common issues that college students face include relationship
worries, situational problems, anxiety, depression, academic concerns,
eating disorders, substance abuse, and identity concerns (Benton, Robertson, Tseng, Newton, & Benton, 2003). In addition to these issues,
diverse students are often expected to adapt to the campus culture,
something that can be detrimental to their mental health. The authors
of this chapter believe that the campus itself should be encouraged to
adapt to diverse students, by changing curricula and pedagogy, promoting cross-cultural competence in faculty and staff members, and implementing specialized services to serve student needs. Therefore, in addition to addressing the needs of these four diverse student populations,
this chapter will also consider the role a campus may inadvertently play
in a system of oppression (e.g., Young, 1990; Bell, 1997), and how that
impacts the mental health functioning of diverse students. Sue (2003)
and Helms (1995) are helpful resources for faculty and staff members
who wish to address their own identities and internalized attitudes
that may affect actions toward diverse populations, especially people of
color.

Students of Color

Although the proportion of students of color attending colleges
has increased, their numbers continue to lag behind those of White

students, with many of the students of color attending two-year colleges (American Council on Education, 2005). Furthermore, the graduation rates for students of color from four-year colleges are lower (e.g., 9.7% of Hispanics vs. 29.6% of Whites, Melendez, 2004). Social and environmental factors, such as lack of social support and discomfort with the college or university social climate, are associated with lower graduation rates for African American students attending primarily White institutions (Gloria, Robinson Kurpius, Hamilton, & Wilson, 1999).

In addition to academic transition, minority students face the challenge of managing and coping with psychological distress as they negotiate the campus milieu (Jones, Castellanos, & Cole, 2002). Intervention at the institutional level is necessary to continue the mission of racial diversity on college and university campuses. Hurtado and Carter (1997) defined institutional climate along four dimensions: (1) the historical legacy of the institution's inclusion and exclusion criteria for students of color, (2) numerical representation of minorities, (3) the psychological climate for these students, and (4) the behavioral climate, typified by the nature of relationships between the various groups on campus.

Some institutions have provided services to students through multicultural centers, which are an avenue whereby the institution can demonstrate the universities' position toward diversity, creating an environment that acknowledges, respects, and enhances multiculturalism (Jones et al., 2002). Often these centers provide the emotional and financial resources for programming various academic, social, and political events. The center should be located at a prominent spot accessible to all students, where center staff can collaborate with other student services departments. In addition, the cross-cultural center's mission should be prominently espoused at student orientation, to communicate its importance for the entire institution.

Although separate ethnic/racial student centers provide students a safe place to congregate and share experiences, those associations may alienate biracial students or students with multiple minority identities. Therefore, student associations should collaborate to sponsor joint diversity conferences/summits, develop a multicultural campus newspaper, create a cultural library, and so forth.

Students of color are often reluctant to seek assistance from mental health counseling or health services. Counseling center staff can develop liaison relationships with multicultural groups (e.g., black student organizations) and provide outreach services where members congregate on campus. Such outreach will enhance the relevance of mental health programs by providing a feedback loop to discern the needs and issues of greatest important to students (Falconer & Hays, 2006).

Gloria et al. (1999) found that student retention was higher if students of color believed that at least one faculty or staff member was interested in their academic progress. Because role models and mentors are critical for students of color, institutions must make it a priority to recruit and retain faculty of color. Such mentors model achievement and provide access to information students might not receive from other sources. To demonstrate that all faculty and staff are invested in students' academic and professional growth, administrators should provide institution-wide diversity training. Workshops can include, but not be limited to, topics such as: being an ally, having a social identity, examining power and privilege, and stopping oppression. In addition to workshops and retreats, administrators should create contexts for faculty to explore their own cultural experiences and to promote diversity and acceptance.

GAY, LESBIAN, BISEXUAL, TRANSGENDER, AND QUEER STUDENTS

In 2006, the Human Rights Campaign stated that 552 American colleges and universities had sexual orientation as part of their non-discrimination policies and 37 included gender identity (HRC.org, 2006). For gay, lesbian, bisexual, transgender, and queer (GLBTQ) students, many universities and colleges are providing the fundamental policy-based protections necessary for a safe academic environment (McRee and Cooper, 1998). Despite such policies, however, many GLBTQ students continue to experience harassment; omission from campus life; homophobic attitudes from staff, faculty, and students; and exclusion from the system (e.g., Brown, Clarke, Gortmaker, & Robinsom-Keilig, 2004). Such discrimination is compounded for students with multiple minority identities such as religion, race, disability, and so on (Suave, 1997). Campuses thus continue to provide only a "tolerant" climate for the GLBTQ student (Evans, 2000). Meredith and Fassinger (2003) believe students living in such an environment can become fearful of interacting with the institution and disengaged from important campus services necessary for graduation.

Administrators should respond in ways that prevent such problems (Evans & Herriott, 2004; Rhoads, 1997) through an integrative perspective, which connects faculty, staff, residence halls, classrooms, student services, publications, and administrators with each other (Garber, 2002). First, many campuses have GLBTQ Resource Centers that provide a setting for support, safety, and specialized services

(Sanlo, 2000). Second, educational weeks can be created where instructors are encouraged to cover particular topics in their classrooms such as GLBTQ concerns (Little & Marx, 2002). Administrators can encourage faculty to seek funding for research on sexual orientation, gender identity, homophobia, identity development, and other related topics as a necessary field of study (Rhoads, 1995). What is researched is often what is taught.

Also, residence hall directors can assist staff managers in developing environments to create safe living environments. Such tried and true programs as Safe Zone and ALLY, which educate students, faculty, and staff about issues of sexual preference and bias, are effective and straightforward processes to meet this need (Neumann, 2005). In addition, students working for campus publications should be sensitive to GLBTQ students and practice equity in their writing and reporting of student events and campus issues (Schreier, 1995).

Finally, it is vital that administrators speak out against hate speech, desecration of GLBTQ student products (e.g., flyers, exhibits, and so on), and acts of discrimination. However, they must be mindful of the delicate balance between cautioning against discriminatory speech and protecting the First Amendment right to free speech (Essex, 2005). Open letters to campus newspapers, e-mails to faculty and staff, and statements made at public meetings are effective methods to communicate institution policies and to make them "living documents."

INTERNATIONAL STUDENTS

The international student population in the United States has been rising steadily (e.g., Mallinckrodt & Leong, 1992). For example, 12% of master's and 26.7% of doctoral students in higher education are international students (Misra & Castillo, 2004). Although college can be stressful for many students, international students face the added challenges of learning new social values and language in addition to educational preparation (Mori, 2000). Based on surveys of international students (e.g., Mori, 2000), the college or university community may need to implement innovative strategies and policies when working with such students. Faculty and staff may need to adopt different communication styles (Harris & Kayes, 1995). For instance, direct eye contact with someone in authority, especially of the opposite gender, is considered disrespectful in some Asian and Middle Eastern cultures.

Many campuses have a center for internationalization to host visiting scholars and international students. Personnel working in such centers provide help with visas, teach English as a second language, and even provide students the opportunity to socialize with others from their home country. Events that promote various countries indicate to students they are truly welcome at the institution. Faculty advisors and staff within centers for academic resources play a crucial role in providing academic guidance and mentorship.

The college or university counseling center may be a helpful resource for international students with mental health concerns, although some students may be more apt to complain of physical problems than emotional difficulties due to various cultural stigmas. Staff at the counseling center should thus partner with health center personnel to address these issues.

Because international students interact with a wide variety of people across campus, all staff and faculty members should provide a culturally respectful and welcoming environment. It would be impractical to ensure that all employees understand all cultures or speak all languages, but basic information about international students and their cultures should be provided via handouts, Web sites, and classes or workshops. In addition, faculty and staff should combat bias toward foreigners that is perhaps even more common in the United States since September 11, 2001.

STUDENT ATHLETES

Although some might assume that athletes are better adjusted and possess higher self-esteem or confidence than other students, and therefore are less likely to experience mental health issues, in fact, student athletes experience the full range of mental health concerns found in the general student population (Donahue, 2004). Athletic participation does not protect student athletes from the stresses of student life; rather it poses additional demands (Etzel, Ferrante, & Pinkney, 1996). Student athletes must adjust to the intense demands of sport at the next level and the rigors of college academics, and it is common for freshmen collegiate athletes to struggle with this process (Leslie-Toogood, Stoney, Hill, & Hughes, 2005). In addition, student-athletes may have concerns with their performance, have trouble accepting their role on the team, have conflicts with coaches or teammates, or lose passion for their sport. Other unique challenges include finding time for social activities, experiencing intense pressure to succeed, dealing with public scrutiny, coping with injuries, and transitioning out of sport at the end of their athletic careers (Nishimoto, 1997; Parham, 1993).

Student athletes may be under pressure from coaches, parents, peers, and sport culture to maintain a certain body weight or shape, and this pressure contributes to the possibility that they will develop disordered eating practices (Andersen, 1992; Otis, Drinkwater, Johnson, Loucks, & Wilmore, 1997; Petrie & Rogers, 2001). Further, this population may use substances to celebrate a win, to deal with the pressure of athletics, or to cope with the trauma of an injury (Leichliter, Meilman, Presley, & Cashin, 1998; Nelson & Wechsler, 2001). Because the role of the collegiate athlete is often an integral part of the student athlete's identity, the transition out of athletics can also have significant implications for mental health (Baillie & Danish, 1992; Brewer, Van Raalte, & Linder, 1993; Kleiber, Greendorfer, Blinde, & Samdahl, 1987; Pearson & Petitpas, 1990; Wooten, 1994). This is particularly true for student athletes who are sidelined by severe injuries and those who have not adequately planned for a future after sport (Murphy, Petitpas, & Brewer, 1996; Taylor and Ogilvie, 1994).

Student athletes must contend with preconceived notions that professors and fellow students might hold, and they are concerned about how other's perceptions of them may affect their experience in higher education (Leslie-Toogood et al., 2005). A student athlete might be considered both a "dunce" and a "hero" on the same campus (Howard-Hamilton & Watt, 2001). Administration, professors, coaches, and other students may see them as an over-privileged "problem" group (Nelson, 1983). Research has found that non-athletes and faculty tend to hold negative stereotypes about the academic motivation and abilities of student athletes (Engstrom & Sedlacek, 1991; Engstrom, Sedlacek, & McEwen, 1995).

Given these stereotypes, problems in this population may go unnoticed, or be subject to unique elements of the student athlete culture leading to barriers in service delivery. Athletes do not often seek mental health services (Bergandi & Wittig, 1984) because of earlier advice to "suck it up" and the strong stigma in the world of sport associated with seeking help for emotional issues. The high profile of student athletes may magnify the attention paid on campus when an athlete seeks help, and on a practical level, student athletes often lack time for counseling. As a result, many athletes suffer in silence, perhaps without the knowledge that help is available or the perspective that seeking help is actually a sign of strength. Athletic support services are readily available to the athlete, but mental health services are often housed in a separate department. Student athletes have been described as "functionally, psychologically, and physically separated from the general student body" (Howard-Hamilton & Watt, 2001). Thus, they may experience a sense of isolation on campus that makes it difficult for them to connect with people outside the athletic world or utilize services. Athletes who do reach out for help will most likely initially seek support from familiar faces they trust within the athletic world. They may talk to teammates, coaches, athletic trainers, or strength coaches about their concerns.

When an athlete is admitted to a college or university, this individual becomes the responsibility not just of the athletic department but also of the institution. It is important to take the time to develop relationships with student athletes before a crisis arises and to develop liaisons with various resources on campuses. A growing number of athletic departments are hiring psychologists, housed within sport medicine or academic advising/counseling departments, to treat mental health issues. Counseling centers are also being utilized at many schools. Student athletes may see a specific counselor who serves as a liaison to the athletic department, or they may be treated by any staff person in the same way non-athletes would be assisted. Other athletic departments are referring student-athletes to an external consultant. It can be useful for college or university administrators to reach out to athletic advisors as well as student-athlete leaders to provide information about services provided by various departments. In addition, departments themselves may need education about student athletes, including debunking myths and promoting sensitivity to the unique issues faced by this population. When providing diversity training on campus, including a discussion about student athletes can be helpful.

Athletes respond best to people who are interested in them in a positive and unobtrusive way (Petitpas & Champagne, 1988) and who do not become fans. As Cogan and Petrie (1996) point out, one must earn their trust and respect by spending time in their space and becoming available to them. Mental health professionals must tread carefully when dealing with issues of confidentiality. If a coach or trainer refers the athlete for services, they will probably want extensive follow up. Clarifying information with the student athlete and obtaining signed releases of information are essential for building trust with the client while maintaining positive relationships with referral sources.

The department of athletics cannot service all the student-athlete needs. Faculty and staff have many things to offer this population, and all are essential for the maintenance of the student-athletes' mental health. Staff can meet the mental health needs of student athletes by becoming familiar with the culture of athletics on campus and fostering positive environments for student athletes.

CONCLUSION

Administrators are in a unique position on campus and thus are able to influence the campus climate in ways other staff and faculty members cannot. By learning about oppression and privilege, by understanding more about diverse groups of students, by revising policies and procedures, by creatively developing options for students, and by being willing to take leadership in educating other staff and faculty, college and university administrators can affect the ways in which students are recruited and retained, and will also ensure that diversity continues to thrive on their campus.

REFERENCES

Andersen, A. E. (1992). Eating disorders in males: A special case? In *Eating, Body Weight and Performance in Athletes: Disorders of Modern Society*, K. D. Brownell, J. Rodin, and J. H. Wilmore (Eds.). Philadelphia: Lea and Febiger, 72-190.

American Council on Education (2005). Minorities in higher education twenty-first annual status report (2003–2004). Washington, DC: Author.

Baillie, P. H. F., & Danish, S. J. (1992). Understanding the career transition of athletes. *The Sport Psychologist, 6*, 77-98.

Bell, L. A. (1997). Theoretical foundations for social justice education. In A. Adams, L. A. Bell, & P. Griffin (Eds.), *Teaching for diversity and social justice: A sourcebook.* Routledge: New York and London.

Benton, S., Robertson, J., Tseng, W., Newton, F., & Benton, S. (2003). Changes in counseling center client problems across 13 years. *Professional Psychology: Research and Practice, 34*, 66-72.

Bergandi, T., & Wittig, A. (1984). Availability of attitudes towards counseling services for the collegiate athlete. *Journal of College Student Personnel, 25*, 557-558.

Brewer, B. W., Van Raalte, J. L., & Linder, D. E. (1993). Athletic identity: Hercules' muscles or Achilles Heel? *International Journal of Sport Psychology, 24*, 237-254.

Brown, R. D., Clarke, B., Gortmaker, V., & Robinson-Keilig, R.

(2004). Assessing the campus climate for gay, lesbian, bisexual, and transgender (GLBT) students using a multiple perspectives approach. *Journal of College Student Development, 45*(1), 8-26.

Cogan, K. D., & Petrie, T. A. (1996). Consultation with college student-athletes. *College Student Journal, 30*, 9-16.

Donohue, B., Covassin, T., Lancer, K., Dickens, Y., Miller, A., Hash, A., & Genet, J. (2004). Examination of psychiatric symptoms in student athletes. *Journal of General Psychology, 131*, 29-35.

Engstrom, C. M., & Sedlacek, W. E. (1991). A study of prejudice toward university student-athletes. *Journal of Counseling and Student Development, 70*, 189-193.

Engstrom, C. M., Sedlacek, W. E., & McEwen, M. K. (1995). Faculty attitudes toward male revenue and non-revenue student-athletes. *Journal of College Student Development, 36*, 217-227.

Essex, N. L. (2005). Gay issues and students' freedom of expression: Is there a lawsuit in your future? *American Secondary Education, 34*(10), 40-47.

Etzel, E. F., Ferrante, A. P., & Pinkney, J. W. (1996). *Counseling college student-athletes: Issues and interventions (2nd Edition)*. Morgantown, WV: Fitness Information Technology.

Evans, N. J., & Herriott, T. K. (2004). Freshman impressions: How investigating the campus climate for LGBT students affected four freshmen students. *Journal of College Student Development, 45*(3), 316-332.

Evans, N. J. (2000). Creating a positive learning environment for gay, lesbian, and bisexual students. In M. B. Baxter Magdolda (Ed.), *Teaching to promote intellectual and personal maturity: Incorporating students' worldviews and identity into the learning process* (New Directions of Teaching No. 32, pp. 81-87). San Francisco: Jossey-Bass.

Falconer, J. W. & Hays, K. A. (2006). Influential factors regarding the career development of African American college students. *Journal of College Development, 32*(3), 219-233.

Garber, L. (2002). Weaving a wide net: The benefits of integrating campus projects to combat homophobia. In E.P. Cramer (Ed.), *Addressing homophobia and heterosexism on college campuses.* New York: The Haworth Press.

Gloria, A. M., Robinson Kurpius, S. E., Hamilton, K. D., & Wilson, M. S. (1999). African American students' persistence at a predominantly white university: Influences of social support, university comfort and self-beliefs. *Journal of College Student Development, 40,* 257-268.

Gruber, C. (2003). What every academic advisor should know about advising student athletes. *The Journal of the National Academic Advising Association, 23*(1), 44-49.

Harris, Z. M., & Kayes, P. (1995). *Multicultural and International Challenges to the Community College: A Model for College-Wide Proactive Response.* U.S.; Paper presented at the Annual Convention of the American Association of Community Colleges, Minneapolis, Minnesota.

Helms, J. E. (1995). An update of Janet Helms' white and people of color racial identity models. In J. G. Ponterotto, J. M. Cases, L. A. Suzuki, & E. M. Alexander (Eds.), *Handbook of multicultural counseling*. Thousand Oaks, CA: Sage Publications.

Howard-Hamilton, M. F., & Watt, S. K. (2001). Student services for athletes. San Francisco: Jossey-Bass.

Human Rights Campaign (2006). Work Life. Retrieved 14, 2006 from http://hrc.org/Template.cfm?Section=Search_the_Database&Template=/CustomSource/WorkNet/srch_list.cfm.

Hurtado, S., & Carter, D. (1997). Effects of college transition and perceptions of campus racial climate on Latino students' sense of belonging. *Sociology of Education, 70,* 324-345.

Jones, L. Castellanos, J., & Cole, D. (2002). Examining the ethnic minority student experience at predominantly white institutions: A case study. *Journal of Hispanic Higher Education, 1*(1), 19-39.

Kleiber, D., Greendorfer, S., Blinde, E. M., & Samdahl, D. (1987). Quality of exit from university sports and life satisfaction in early adulthood. *Sociology of Sport Journal, 4,* 28-36.

Little, P., & Marx, M. (2002). Teaching about heterosexism and creating an empathic experience of homophobia. In E.P. Cramer (Ed.), *Addressing homophobia and heterosexism on college campuses.* New York: The Haworth Press.

Leichliter, J. S., Meilman, P. W., Presley, C. A., & Cashin, J. R. (1998). Alcohol use and related consequences among students with varying levels of involvement in college athletics. *Journal of American College Health, 46,* 257-262.

Leslie-Toogood, S. A., Stoney, B., Hill, R., & Hughes, P. (2005, March). Best Practices for Student Affairs Professionals in Working with College Student-Athletes: Learning from the Athletes Themselves. National Association of Student Personnel Administrators Annual Conference, Tampa.

Mallinckrodt, B., & Leong, F. T. L. (1992). International graduate students, stress, and social support. *Journal of Counseling and Development, 33,* 21-25.

McRee, T. K., & Cooper, D. L. (1998). Campus environments for gay, lesbian, and bisexual students at southeastern institutions of higher education. *NASPA Journal, 36,* 48-60.

Melendez, S. (2004). From humble beginnings come great achievements. In American Council on Education, *Reflections on 20 years of minorities in higher education and the ACE annual status report.* Washington, DC: American Council on Education.

Meredith, M. J., & Fassinger, R. E. (2003). Career development, lesbian identity development, and campus climate among lesbian college students. *Journal of College Student Development, 44*(6), 845-860.

Misra, R., & Castillo, L. G. (May, 2004). Academic stress among College Students: Comparisons of American and International students. *International Journal of Stress Management, 11*(2), 132-148.

Mori, S. C. (2000). Addressing the mental health concerns of international students. *Journal of counseling and development, 78,* 137-144.

Murphy, G. M., Petitpas, A. J., & Brewer, B. W. (1996). Identity foreclosure, athletic identity, and career maturity in intercollegiate athletes. *The Sport Psychologist, 10,* 239-246.

Nelson, E. S. (1983). How the myth of the dumb jock becomes fact: A developmental of counselors. *Counseling and Values, 27,* 176-185.

Nelson, T. F., & Wechsler, H. (2001). Alcohol and college athletes. *Medicine and Science in Sports and Exercise, 33,* 43-47.

Neumann, S. L. (2005). Creating a safe zone for sexual minority students in the psychology classroom. *Teaching of Psychology, 32*(2), *121-123.*

Nishimoto, P. A. (1997). Touchdowns and term papers: Telescoping the college student-athlete culture. *College Student Affairs Journal, 16*(2), 96-103.

Otis, C. L., Drinkwater, B., Johnson, M., Loucks, A., & Wilmore, J. (1997). ACSM position stand: The female athlete triad. *Medicine and Science in Sports and Exercise, 29,* i-ix.

Parham, W. D. (1993). The intercollegiate athlete: A 1990s profile. *The Counseling Psychologist, 21*(3), 411-429.

Pearson, R., & Petitpas, A. (1990). Transitions of athletes: Developmental and preventive perspectives. *Journal of Counseling and Development, 69,* 7-10.

Petipas, A., & Champagne, D. E. (1988). Developmental programming for intercollegiate athletes. *Journal of College Student Development, 29,* 454-459.

Petrie, T. A., & Rogers, R. (2001). Extending the discussion of eating disorders to include men and athletes. The *Counseling Psychologist, 29,* 743-753.

Rhoads, R. A. (1997). Implications of the growing visibility of gay and bisexual male students on campus. *NASPA Journal, 34*(4), 275-286.

Rhoads, R. A. (1995, January 27). The campus climate for gay students who leave the closet. *Chronicle of Higher Education,* A56.

Sanlo, R. L. (2000). The LGBT campus resource center director: The new profession in student affairs. *NASPA Journal, 37*(3), 485-495.

Schreier, B. A. (1995). Moving beyond tolerance: A new paradigm for programming about homophobia and heterosexism. *Journal of College Student Development, 36,* 19-26.

Sauve, J. R. (1997, October). I ride the bus on the other side of the street: The coming-out experiences of black gay men in college. *Dissertation Abstracts International: Section B: The Sciences and Engineering.* Vol 58(4-B), 2137.

Sue, D. W. (2003). *Overcoming our racism: The journey to liberation.* San Francisco: Jossey-Bass.

University of California Regents v Bakke (1978) 438 U.S. 265.

Taylor, J., & Ogilvie, B. C. (1994). A conceptual model of adaptation to retirement among athletes. *Journal of Applied Sport Psychology, 6,* 1-20.

Wooten, H. R. (1994). Cutting losses for student-athletes in transition: An integrative transition model. *Journal of Employment Counseling, 31,* 2-9.

Young, I. M. (1990) *Justice and the politics of difference.* Princeton, NJ: Princeton University Press.

CHAPTER 10

Responding to the College Student Mental Health Problem

Sherry A. Benton and Stephen L. Benton

The Center for Disease Control and Prevention defines an epidemic as "the occurrence of cases of an illness in a community or region which is in excess of the number of cases normally expected for that disease in that area at that time" (CDC Web site, 2006). If depression, anxiety, and suicidal ideation were infectious diseases, they would easily be considered epidemics on today's college and university campuses. Accordingly, in a July 2006 press release, the American Medical Association called for improved mental health services on campuses: "Among college students, depression and related mental illnesses are significant, growing problems and contribute to self-harm and suicide. Existing campus counseling and health services are often overburdened due to inadequate resources as severe mental health conditions increase among students (AMA Board Member J. James Rohack, M.D.).

Although most student affairs personnel recognize the increased prevalence of these problems on campuses, finding resources to address the problems is a challenge. Some college and university administrators have wondered what their responsibility for student mental health problems should be. How do mental health services fit within the academic mission of the institution? The answer to the question is that a close relationship exists between the severity of students' mood disorders/psychological problems and students' academic and social functioning. Figure 10.1 portrays a positive linear relationship between students' self-reported mood difficulties/anxiety and their self-reported ratings of how their mental health problems have interfered with academic and social functioning (Benton, 2004). As mood difficulties and anxiety increase, students report having more severe interference. Furthermore, mood difficulties explain 25% of the variance in learning problems (Robertson et al., 2006). Mental health problems are, therefore, directly and adversely associated with academic difficulties.

Figure 10.1. College Students' Scores on Mood/Anxiety Scale and Levels of Interference with Social and Academic Functioning.

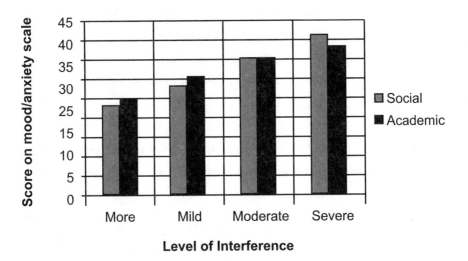

Source: Kansas State University, Counseling Services, Annual report, 2005.

The authors of the preceding chapters have argued convincingly that a campus-wide support network, along with good mental health services, can improve students' academic performance and, ultimately, retention and graduation. In this concluding chapter, we summarize the authors' main points within the context of the five goals stated in the introductory chapter.

1. Help college and university administrators to gain an understanding of the scope of mental health problems on college and university campuses.

In the previous chapters, the authors have cited multiple sources of evidence that indicate the prevalence of mental health problems among college and university students has increased at alarming rates over the past 20 years. The longitudinal prevalence data collected at Kansas State University indicate that the proportion of students with anxiety disorders and depression has tripled over the past 17 years. The annual National College Health Association surveys indicate that anxiety and depression have increased annually from 2000 through 2005, with 45.7% of the students in spring 2005 reporting that they felt so depressed they could not function.

2. Help college and university administrators to understand the legal issues associated with students with mental health problems.

In Chapter 3, Dickerson presented a comprehensive view of the legal issues associated with students with mental health issues. She began with three legal implications for admission decisions:

1. If a college or university has reasonable concerns about the safety of a potential student and others on campus, it may deny admission or require the applicant to provide additional information about the disability and its impact.

2. A college or university can ask about past criminal activity even if it is related to a student's disability.

3. In certain special programs where the well-being of others is at stake, a college or university can request the results of psychological examinations as part of the admissions process.

With regard to already admitted students with disabilities, which would include mental health disabilities, admissions-related tests and activities must reasonably accommodate the needs of disabled students. The college or university is expected to (a) help students understand their rights and responsibilities, (b) develop disability awareness plans, and (c) create an environment that minimizes stigma and increases the acceptance of students with disabilities.

Confidentiality of student records is also an important area of legal attention. The challenge is to find a balance between maintaining student confidentially and promoting campus safety. Some campus personnel such as psychologists, campus ministers, and mental health workers have more stringent ethical expectations than others. In addition, HIPAA, FERPA, state statutes, and other professional ethical codes are important considerations.

Student suicide threats and attempts have received extensive media attention. From a legal perspective, college and university staff owe students "a reasonable duty of care to protect them from foreseeable harm" (Dickerson, 2006). To determine what is meant by "reasonable" and "foreseeable," administrators should form collaborative risk-management teams that identify risks and solutions for minimizing them, educate others about those risks, and regularly evaluate the solutions.

With regard to discipline issues, when dealing with students with disabilities, the focus should be on the student's behavior rather than on the disability. Education, values, and principles—not sanctions and punishment—should be the primary goals of the discipline system.

Colleges and universities legally may deny applications for readmission from disabled students when (a) the institution is not aware of the disability, (b) readmission is denied on the same grounds that would have been used for a similarly situated non-disabled student, or (c) the former student is not an "otherwise qualified person," taking into consideration the disability and all other relevant factors. Courts are particularly deferential to an institution's decision not to readmit when the safety of the applicant, other students, faculty, and members of the campus community are legitimately at risk—as supported by professional assessments in the file—and when the faculty exercises non-discriminatory academic judgment.

3. Provide theoretical frameworks and practical strategies for supplying comprehensive and integrated services for students with mental health problems.

Authors in this volume presented three theoretical frameworks that can be used to develop services for students with mental health problems. Owen, Tao, and Rodolfa described the *Cube model*, which recommends collaborative, campus-wide strategic planning, institutional-level policies and procedures, a clear system of communication between campus members, and protection of student privacy. All members of a campus community should be involved at some level, including peers, faculty, administrators, and staff. The cube model describes multiple levels of intervention that include both primary prevention to keep problems from becoming worse or from interfering with academics and secondary prevention to develop coordinated services when a problem develops.

In her chapter on legal issues, Dickerson described the facilitator model, initially developed by Lake and Bickel (1999). The facilitator model begins with the premise that traditional university and college students are still developing mentally, socially, and physically. Therefore, the college or university takes a developmental approach to students. The institution takes reasonable care to create an environment where students can make reasonable choices. The university or college does not attempt to control the students but empowers them to make choices for themselves within a structured environment.

In Chapter 4, Newton described the AISP model (Assessment Intervention of Student Problems, Delworth, 1999) as a means for providing mental health consultation for urgent and emergent care. The model recommends that student affairs professionals begin by setting policies and procedures, specifying protocols, identifying resources, and identifying consultants with expertise. When responding to a crisis or incident on campus, administrators and staff should follow due process procedures. Collaboration among the many offices on campus is essential, and flexibility should be allowed in adapting to the unique circumstances of each individual and situation. The Jed Foundation's "Framework for Developing Institutional Protocols for the Acutely Distressed or Suicidal College Student" can be an excellent resource for developing campus protocols (http://www.jedfoundation.org/framework. php).

4. Provide more specific theory, strategies and ideas for relevant student affairs offices.

Benton, Benton, and Perl discussed theory and strategies relevant for academic faculty. Faculty can often serve as the gatekeepers for students with mental health problems. Frequently, faculty are the first to notice changes in students, and with some training they can respond properly and refer students to appropriate services. The authors also distinguished between (a) student mental health problems that can be remediated and would not interfere with functioning in professional roles and (b) student competence problems that need to be addressed.

Osfield and Junco provided a useful summary of mental health categories and accommodations for a wide array of mental health problems. They stressed that students with disabilities are looking for equal and fair treatment and that, with appropriate accommodations, faculty and student affairs professionals can create an environment relatively free of barriers to the success of students with disabilities.

Cooper discussed challenging issues faced by counseling centers today. These included balancing increased client demand with tightening budgets and struggling to meet the needs for clinical services, prevention, and outreach efforts on campus. These combined pressures lead to issues of self-care and burnout for counseling center staff.

Moses described environmental and social influences on student health and well-being. She described the Public Health Model as an effective approach for providing a healthy campus community to prevent the development of many mental health problems.

5. Help administrators to understand the unique needs of some populations on campus.

The chapter on diversity issues identified several populations likely to have unique needs and problems associated with accessing services. Populations discussed included racial and ethnic groups, international students, and student athletes.

Having spoken with administrators and staff on many college and university campuses across the United States during the last several years, the first author of this chapter (Sherry A. Benton) has found that most student affairs professionals are genuinely concerned about student mental health problems. They are also trying to provide the best services possible, given budget limitations. In her consulting with professionals, she has noticed vast differences in institutional approaches to student mental health problems. At one university with a strong and proactive vice-president for student affairs, there were clear objectives, strategic planning, and a cohesive and comprehensive approach to students with mental health problems. At another university, the vice president for student affairs told her that the institution's high academic standards made concerns about retention, graduation, and student mental health irrelevant. The vice president believed that students were easily replaced with others eager to be admitted. This cavalier approach to students might have created an uncaring environment that left students with few resources for coping with mental health issues. These two examples show the wide range that exists on college and university campuses in attitudes and services available for student mental health services.

Throughout this book, the various authors have tried to provide theory, practical strategies, and specific examples to help college and university administrators, faculty, and staff to reflect upon their approaches to mental health problems with their students. Our hope is that colleges and universities will develop their own teams for strategic planning, examine issues of stigma on their campuses, and improve access and availability of appropriate mental health services.

REFERENCES

Benton, S. A. (2006). The scope and context of the problem. In Benton, S. A., and Benton, S. L. (Eds.), *Student Mental Health: Effective Services and Strategies Across Campus.* Washington, DC: NASPA.

Benton, S. A. (2005) *Using Data to inform Clinical Mental Health Services Planning, Development and Evaluation.* Effective Interventions for Student Mental Health on Campus: Collaboration and Community. Co-sponsored by the National Association of Student Personnel Administrators (NASPA), National College Health Association (NCHA), and The Chickering Group, Providence, RI.

Benton, S. A., Benton, S. L., Newton, F. B., Benton, K. L., and Robertson, J. M. (2004). Changes in client problems: Contributions and limitations from a 13-year study. *Professional Psychology: Research and Practice, 35*, 317-319.

Benton, S. L., Benton, S. A., and Perl, M. (2006). Key issues for faculty regarding college mental health. In Benton, S. A., and Benton, S. L. (Eds.), *Student Mental Health: Effective Services and Strategies Across Campus.* Washington, DC: NASPA.

Bickel, R. & Lake, P. (1999). *The Rights and Responsibilities of the Modern University: Who Assumes the Risks of College Life?* Durham, North Carolina: Carolina Academic Press.

Brent, M. E., Cornish, J. A. E., Leslie-Toogood, A., Nadkami, L. I., and Schreier, B. A. (2006). Special populations: diversity on campus. . In Benton, S. A., and Benton, S. L. (Eds.), *Student*

Mental Health: Effective Services and Strategies Across Campus. Washington, DC: NASPA.

Center for Disease Control and Prevention Web site, (2006). http://www.cdc.gov/epo/dphsi/casedef/definition_of_terms.htm.

College Health Association. (2005b). American College Health Association-National College Health Assessment: Reference Group Executive Summary Spring 2005. Baltimore: American College Health Association.

Cooper, S. E. (2006). Counseling and mental health services. In Benton, S. A., and Benton, S. L. (Eds.), *Student Mental Health: Effective Services and Strategies Across Campus.* Washington, DC: NASPA.

Dickerson, D. (2006). Legal issues for campus administrators, faculty, and staff. In Benton, S. A., and Benton, S. L. (Eds.), *Student Mental Health: Effective Services and Strategies Across Campus.* Washington, DC: NASPA.

Delworth, U. (1989). The AISP Model: Assessment-Intervention of Student Problems. In U. Delworth (Ed.), *Dealing with the Behavioral and Psychological Problems of students. New Directions for Student Services, 45,* 3-14. San Francisco: Jossey-Bass.

JED Foundation. (2006). Framework for developing institutional protocols for the acutely distressed or suicidal college student http://www.jedfoundation.org/framework.php.

Moses, K.S., (2006). Health education and Health services and college student mental health. In Benton, S. A., and Benton, S.

L. (Eds.), *Student Mental Health: Effective Services and Strategies Across Campus*. Washington, DC: NASPA.

Newton, F. B. (2006). Mental health consultation for urgent and emergent campus issues. In Benton, S. A., and Benton, S. L. (Eds.), *Student Mental Health: Effective Services and Strategies Across Campus*. Washington, DC: NASPA.

Osfield, K. J., and Junco, R. (2006). Services for students with mental health disabilities. In Benton, S. A., and Benton, S. L. (Eds.), *Student Mental Health: Effective Services and Strategies Across Campus*. Washington, DC: NASPA.

Owen, J., Tao, K. and Rodolfa, E. R. (2006). Distressed and distressing students: Creating a campus care community. In Benton, S. A., and Benton, S. L. (Eds.), *Student Mental Health: Effective Services and Strategies Across Campus*. Washington, DC: NASPA.

Robertson, J. M., Benton, S. L., Newton, F. B., Downey, R. G., Marsh, P. A., Benton, S. A., Tseng, W., & Shin, K. (2006). K-State Problem Identification Rating Scale (K-PIRS) for college students. *Measurement and Evaluation in Education, 39,* 141-160.

Rohack, J. J. (June 13, 2006). *AMA calls for more mental health services on college campuses*. American Medical Association Press release.

Contributors

Sherry A. Benton, PhD, ABPP, is associate professor of counseling and educational psychology and assistant director of counseling services at Kansas State University. Her primary research interests are college student mental health and college student drinking. In 2006, she received the Education Advocacy Distinguished Service Award from the American Psychological Association's Board of Educational Affairs for her groundbreaking research on college student mental health.

Stephen L. Benton, PhD, is professor and chair of counseling and educational psychology at Kansas State University. His research interests include cognitive processes involved in academic learning, college student drinking, and college student mental health. He is a fellow in the Division of Educational Psychology of the American Psychological Association (APA), the former editor of *Educational Psychology Review,* and is the recipient of K-State's Excellence in Graduate Faculty Teaching Award.

Megan E. Brent, PhD, is the sport psychologist at the University of Kansas, where she provides individual counseling and performance enhancement services for student athletes. She earned her doctorate in counseling psychology at The Ohio State University and completed an internship and post-doctoral fellowship at Kansas State University's Counseling Services.

Stewart E. Cooper, PhD, ABPP, is director of counseling services and professor of psychology at Valparaiso University in Indiana. Dr. Cooper is a fellow and diplomate in both counseling psychology and consulting psychology, and has leadership roles on the executive boards of both of the associated APA divisions. He has written extensively on college student mental health, prevention, psychometric analysis, substance abuse, dual-career issues, organizational consultation, and sex therapy.

Jennifer A. Erickson Cornish, PhD, is assistant professor and director of clinical training and the internship consortium at the University of Denver Graduate School of Professional Psychology. Her primary research interests are supervision, training, and multiculturalism. She is currently secretary for the Society of Counseling Psychology (APA Division 17) and is the Colorado representative on the APA Council.

Darby Dickerson, JD, is the vice president and dean, and a professor of law, at Stetson University College of Law in St. Petersburg, Florida. She writes in the areas of higher-education law and policy, legal writing and citation, and litigation ethics. She has received Stetson University's Teaching Excellence Award and is the two-time recipient of the University's Homer and Dolly Hand Award for Excellence in Faculty Scholarship.

Reynol Junco, PhD, is an assistant professor in the Department of Academic Development and Counseling and the director of disability services at Lock Haven University of Pennsylvania. His main research interest is student development through the use of technology. He has been invited to present workshops about millennial student culture and technology throughout the United States and Europe.

Karen S. Moses is a registered dietitian and certified health education specialist. She serves as director of wellness and health promotion at Arizona State University, and is currently co-chair of the NASPA Health in Higher Education Knowledge Community. She is a fellow of the American College Health Association, and she received that association's Ollie B. Moten.

Lavita I. Nadkarni, PhD, is an associate professor and director of forensic studies at the University of Denver's Graduate School of Professional Psychology. Her clinical and research interests are in the areas of gender and multicultural issues within the forensic field, and the clinical training of graduate students and interns.

Fred B. Newton, PhD, is a professor of counseling and educational psychology and director of student counseling services at Kansas State University. He has written extensively on the topics of college student mental health, characteristics of college students, peer counseling and intervention strategies, and programs for changing behaviors.

Kenneth J. Osfield, PhD, serves as the Americans with Disabilities Act compliance officer and an instructor in the College of Education student personnel in higher education program at the University of Florida. He is the recipient of the NASPA Region III James E. Scott Mid-Level Student Affairs Professional Award

(2003) and the Region III William Leftwich New Professional
Award (1991).

Jesse J. Owen, PhD, is an assistant professor in the Department
of Counseling Psychology at Gannon University in Erie, Pennsylvania. His research interests include counseling process and outcome,
romantic relationships, and multicultural theory and practice.

Michael F. Perl, PhD, is the assistant dean and director of the
Center for Student and Professional Services in the College of
Education at Kansas State University. His primary research interest
is supervision of practicum experiences.

Emil R. Rodolfa, PhD, is the director of the University of California–Davis Counseling and Psychological Services, where he has
worked since 1988. He is the editor of *Training and Education in
Professional Psychology* and a member of the governing board of
the Association for University and College Counseling Center Directors (AUCCCD). For his extensive contributions to psychology
education and practice, he received the Award for Distinguished
Contributions of Applications of Psychology to Education and
Training from the American Psychological Association.

Barry A. Schreier, PhD, HSPP, is coordinator of training at
Purdue University's Counseling and Psychological Services. He is
president of the Association of Counseling Center Training Agencies (ACCTA) and board member of the Association of Psychology
Postdoctoral and Internship Centers (APPIC). Dr. Schreier pub-

lishes widely on issues related to the lives of people who are gay, lesbian, bisexual, transgender, and queer.

Karen W. Tao, EdM, is a therapist at the University of Wisconsin–Madison Counseling and Consultation Services. Her research interests include academic persistence for students of color in higher education and the impact of the supervisory relationship on multicultural counselor training and development.

Adrienne Leslie-Toogood, PhD, is an assistant professor in the Department of Counseling and Educational Psychology at Kansas State University. The recipient of the 2006 Outstanding Professor Award for NASPA Region IV-West, she has made numerous presentations at scholarly, juried international conferences and has written several publications in peer-reviewed journals and edited books. She is a licensed psychologist in the state of Kansas and has worked as a psychologist and sport psychologist with athletes in both the United States and Canada.